THE EINKORN COOKBOOK

THE EINKORN COOKBOOK

DISCOVER THE WORLD'S PUREST AND MOST ANCIENT FORM OF WHEAT

SHANNA AND TIM MALLON

FAIR WINDS

Quarto is the authority on a wide range of topics.

Quarto educates, entertains and enriches the lives of our readers—enthusiasts and lovers of hands-on living.

www.QuartoKnows.com

First published in the USA in 2015 by
Fair Winds Press, an imprint of
Quarto Publishing Group USA Inc.
100 Cummings Center
Suite 406-L
Beverly, MA 01915-6101
www.QuartoKnows.com
Visit our blogs at www.QuartoKnows.com

ISBN: 978-1-59233-642-5

Digital edition published in 2015
eISBN: 978-1-62788-186-9

Library of Congress Cataloging-in-Publication Data

Mallon, Shanna.

The einkorn cookbook : discover the world's purest and most ancient form of wheat--non-hybridized, easy to digest, nutrient-rich, delicious flavor / Shanna and Tim Mallon.

pages cm

ISBN 978-1-59233-642-5 (paperback)

1. Cooking (Wheat)   2. Wheat--Heirloom varieties.
I. Mallon, Tim.   II. Title.

TX809.W45M35 2014

641.6'311--dc23

2014017893

Cover and book design by www.studioink.co.uk
Photography by Shanna and Tim Mallon

Printed and bound in USA

To the One who gives all good gifts, even our food to eat.

–James 1:17

Contents

Introduction   08

Chapter 1: All About Einkorn   09
Chapter 2: Breakfasts   19
Chapter 3: Breads   43
Chapter 4: Appetizers   71
Chapter 5: Einkorn Berry Salads   85
Chapter 6: Main Dishes   103
Chapter 7: Desserts   135

Resources   168
Acknowledgments   169
About the Authors   170
Index   171

INTRODUCTION

long as we have the resources to buy it and the willingness to try to make something new.

On our blog, Food Loves Writing, and among our friends, it's no secret that we're passionate home cooks. We believe there is beauty and power in discovering ingredients and making your own food, and that's what led us to einkorn a few years ago. Tim had researched the nutritional profile and health benefits of this ancient grain that neither of us grew up eating, and he saw that it had some unique, hard-to-ignore selling points. From the first bag of einkorn flour we purchased to the growing stock of berries and flour that we now keep on hand, we've been repeatedly impressed with the taste, texture, versatility, and digestibility of einkorn.

In this book, we want to showcase these features in a way that prompts you toward your home kitchen with a bag of einkorn by your side. We want to give you confidence to approach this ingredient with anticipation and hope—because we're certain that once you try it, you'll see what we have: Everyone is capable of creating flavorful, nutritious food . . . especially when you start with something good.

The first time we met, it was over gourmet ice pops—Shanna, the pistachio; Tim, the grapefruit—and in the years since, the foods we're eating and the meals we're making have never been far from our minds. We enjoy food and enjoy learning about, experimenting with, and sharing as much of it as we can with the people we love; we're probably not so different from you in that way. Even with all the exciting restaurants and amazing ready-made foods available on the market today, most people are still, night after night, eating homemade meals at the kitchen table. Most of us need and want to create food for ourselves and for the people we love—and we can. Eating good food is possible as

CHAPTER ONE

All About Einkorn

Einkorn may not be a household name today—but that wasn't always the case. An ancient grain with origins dating as far back as 7600 BCE, einkorn has been around as long as wheat has been cultivated. In fact, einkorn wheat is simply the earliest variety of cultivated wheat, also known as *triticum monococcum L.*, which is why it's sometimes referred to as "original wheat." It has a more developed root system than modern wheat, which enables it to uptake more nutrients—lutein, iron, phosphorus, potassium, thiamin, and vitamins A and E, to name a few.

A BRIEF HISTORY OF EINKORN

Throughout history wheat has been cultivated and hybridized to increase yield, increase disease resistance, and develop desirable baking characteristics, such as increased elasticity in the gluten. As new varieties of wheat with these characteristics took over the market, the original einkorn wheat became less well-known.

The hybridization of wheat changed the genetic makeup of what was originally a simpler, more digestible version of the grain. Einkorn, for example, is what's called a diploid (i.e., made up of two complete sets of chromosomes) and contains fourteen total chromosomes, while later varieties of wheat—such as emmer, kamut, and durum—contain twenty-eight. More modern varieties such as spelt, hard red wheat, and soft white wheat contain even more still, at forty-two

chromosomes. This is significant for a few reasons: First, the more the genetic structure of the grain has been manipulated, the more likely that its proteins—such as the gluten and gliadins found in gluten—can cause intestinal distress. In the 2010 Springer *Theoretical and Applied Genetics*, for example, it was shown that modern wheat breeding practices may have led to an increased exposure to celiac disease epitopes (the part of the molecule that causes the body to attack it via an antibody). Second, the genetic changes that wheat has undergone have affected the way the plant takes up nutrients from the soil, resulting in less nutrients in the final product. This means that einkorn, being nonhybridized, has the distinct advantage of being both easier on the digestive tract, and more nutritionally dense.

WHY COOK WITH EINKORN

There are many reasons we love cooking and baking with einkorn. First, as we've talked about, einkorn is the most nutritious of the wheat varieties and easier to digest than others. It naturally contains more protein and has a different gluten structure than other varieties of wheat. It is rich in beta-carotene, vitamin A, lutein, and riboflavin. What's more, it lacks the D genome present in modern wheat, a factor that is of note since significant, potentially harmful structural changes to the gluten in wheat were introduced through the D genome. In addition, a 2006 study in the *Scandinavian Journal of Gastroenterology* showed einkorn

lacked toxicity from one component of gluten, based on biopsies of the intestinal lining of celiac patients.

Beside its health advantages, we simply enjoy the taste of einkorn (and other ancient and heirloom varietals). Growing up, neither of us was exposed to many different types of grains or seeds, and now we find that these ancient and heirloom varieties are not only some of the most nutritious options available on the market, but also they are incredibly delicious. By using these varieties, we can better nourish our families, raise awareness about food diversity, and help preserve traditional foodways for future generations.

USING EINKORN IN YOUR KITCHEN

While einkorn is in the same family as farro, spelt, and traditional wheat, it does not behave exactly like any of these grains in baking and cooking. Cooked einkorn berries are slightly chewier, for example, and the flavor is deeper and richer. What's more, the flour reacts with liquids differently than regular flour, absorbing less and generally more slowly. Our recipes take these differences into account, of course, but if you want to adapt your own recipes to using einkorn, try keeping these tips in mind and be forgiving if things don't go as planned!

WHAT'S IN A NAME?

Thanks to its rich history, einkorn goes by various names. Among them are *farro piccolo* (Italian), *shippon* (Hebrew), and *le petit épeautre* (French). In English, an einkorn "berry" refers to the whole kernel, or grain (similar to "wheat berries").

USING EINKORN FLOUR

There are two main kinds of einkorn flour on the market today: whole-grain and white all-purpose. While both are made from the same einkorn berries, the whole-grain version retains all the bran and germ, while the white has had most of the bran and germ removed, allowing for a lighter product that keeps longer. Flour made at home, either by grinding berries in a grain mill or in another processor, is whole-grain einkorn flour. There is also sprouted einkorn flour, as well as the possibility of sprouting and then grinding your own flour at home (see page 14).

Note that recipes that call for whole-grain einkorn flour will be hearty, dense, and slightly nutty; recipes that call for white, all-purpose einkorn flour will be lighter and more delicate. It is always possible to swap one type out for the other using the same one-to-one weight, but results will vary, and recipes that call for yeast are especially sensitive. For this reason, we provide notations on recipes where swapping is particularly difficult.

EINKORN FLOUR WEIGHTS

For reference, here are the various weights of different types of einkorn flour. Note that sifted einkorn flour is whole-grain flour that has been run through a sifter, with the strained bran discarded, and then weighed.

Whole-Grain Einkorn Flour = 110 g per cup
Sifted Whole-Grain Einkorn Flour = 100 g per cup
White, All-Purpose Einkorn Flour = 125 g per cup

BUYING AND STORING EINKORN

While some natural groceries carry einkorn, the current best place to buy einkorn berries or einkorn flour is online. See our Resources section on page 168 for a full list of our preferred brands.

In terms of flour specifically, Jovial Foods (JovialFoods.com) offers all-purpose einkorn flour, a high-extraction flour with most of its germ and bran removed; this option results in a lighter texture and more delicate crumb in baked goods. Whole-grain einkorn flour, is available online from Breadtopia, Tropical Traditions, Simple Origins, GrowSeed.org, Einkorn.com, and others—and you can often find online coupon codes, free shipping deals, and bulk offers from these places in order to save money. It is also possible to make at home by grinding berries yourself in a grain mill. If you would like finer flour, you can sift your freshly ground flour with a fine mesh metal strainer to separate the bran.

As anyone who's purchased grains in bulk can tell you, the way you store your grains is important. Without proper storage, both einkorn berries and einkorn flour can become susceptible to insect problems and/or rancidity. After learning this lesson the hard way, we've begun storing all our grains in sealed glass jars instead of paper or plastic. What's more, we usually freeze our grains and flours if space allows.

ECONOMICS OF EINKORN

Compared with other grains, einkorn may seem expensive, but, like a lot of heirloom varieties, we find that its benefits far outweigh its cost. With distinctive nutritional characteristics that have fallen to the wayside in modern varieties, einkorn's cost reflects both this fact and the fact that it is more difficult to harvest. Better for the body, plus unparalleled flavor and taste? For us, that's value we don't mind paying for.

SOAKING AND SPROUTING EINKORN

Just as with most grains, einkorn benefits from soaking and/or sprouting. These processes not only boost the amount of available nutrients, but also help neutralize the anti-nutrient phytic acid, which is found in most grains (and nuts) and is a known culprit for causing gut inflammation and digestion problems. Soaking or culturing flour (such as in traditional sourdough) helps make the final product easier to digest, as the grain has essentially begun to predigest because of the good bacteria in the culture. Sprouting unlocks many of a grain's nutrients as well, essentially allowing it to become a little plant.

Throughout this book, you will notice we always call for soaking einkorn berries and only occasionally call for soaking a flour mixture, due to our personal preferences. However, it is always possible and helpful for aiding digestion if you want to soak or sprout your einkorn each time; just follow the instructions below. Additionally, for more information on soaking, souring, and sprouting, *Nourishing Traditions* by Sally Fallon is an excellent resource.

HOW TO SOAK EINKORN BERRIES

In a bowl, combine berries with enough filtered water to cover them and up to a tablespoon (15ml) of an acidic medium such as apple cider vinegar, whey, or lemon juice. Soak berries for 8 hours (and up to overnight). After soaking, strain and rinse the berries, discarding the water. At this point, they are ready to be cooked or sprouted (see below).

HOW TO SPROUT EINKORN BERRIES

To make your own sprouted einkorn, follow the same process for soaking einkorn berries as above, but after soaking and rinsing, place the berries in either a strainer (covered with a plate), a glass jar, or a sprouter and leave it on the counter, rinsing every 4 to 8 hours. Within 2 days, you should start to see a little white bud appear at the edge of each berry; a tiny sprout is all you're looking for (about 1/8 to 1/4 inch [3 to 6 mm]). As soon as this appears, berries are ready to be strained, rinsed, and cooked, or dried and prepared for grinding into flour (see below).

HOW TO MAKE SPROUTED EINKORN FLOUR

To make your own sprouted flour, sprout your einkorn berries as instructed above, then dehydrate at 150°F (66°C) or below until completely dry. Note that this can take from 12 to 24 hours, depending on your oven or dehydrator; bite down on a kernel to test for dryness—it should be crunchy.

Once done, process the berries in a grain mill or high-speed processor. Use the flour just like you would regular einkorn flour; the resulting consistency will be just like that of whole-grain einkorn flour.

COOKED EINKORN BERRIES

Cooking einkorn berries is pretty simple. We always soak ours the night before cooking, but beyond that the process is quick and easy: Combine with water in a pot, bring to a simmer, cook until al dente. We've found we tend to cook our berries longer than most people would because we like them a little softer, but the doneness is up to you.

Yield: 2¼ cups (428 g) cooked einkorn berries

1 cup (200 g) einkorn berries
1 teaspoon apple cider vinegar

* In a medium bowl, combine einkorn berries, apple cider vinegar, and enough water to cover the berries by an inch (2.5 cm). Cover bowl, and let sit at room temperature for 8 hours or overnight. Afterward, rinse and drain berries and place in a 2.5- or 3-quart (2.5 or 3 L) stockpot with 1½ cups (350 ml) of water. Bring mixture to a boil over medium heat; reduce to a simmer; cook for 30 to 40 minutes, until al dente. Berries may be used immediately in soups, salads, or other recipes. They may also be stored in an airtight container in the refrigerator for up to 2 weeks.

A NOTE ABOUT GLUTEN IN EINKORN

Gluten consists of the proteins gliadin and glutenin, the two of which give bread dough its elasticity. Einkorn contains just as much gluten as other varieties of wheat, but it has a more favorable ratio of gliadin to glutenin, and, due to its simple genetic structure, it is tolerated by many who would otherwise be unable to eat modern wheat. While some studies have shown that einkorn digests more easily than other wheat varieties, and that it has a lack of gliadin toxicity, it is best that individuals with celiac or extreme gluten sensitivities refrain, while those with a mild gluten intolerance or sensitivity may experiment.

INGREDIENTS AND SUGGESTED SUBSTITUTIONS

We've written this cookbook to be reflective of the way we cook in our kitchen and the ingredients we use, while also being adaptable to others' needs and pantries. Here is a quick rundown of less common ingredients you can expect to see in our recipes, with short explanations of what they are and how you might replace them. Most of these products are available at natural foods stores or online. For more information, see the Resources section.

COCONUT OIL

Coconut oil is a wonder product extracted from the kernel of mature coconuts, and it has many uses even beyond food. In this book, we use extra-virgin organic coconut oil to roast vegetables and as a fat in baking because of its stability as a saturated fat, its beneficial lauric acid content, and its healthful medium chain triglycerides (MCTs).

There are many brands of coconut oil on the market today, each with its own aroma, texture, and taste, so experiment to find which you like best. In general, we enjoy the light taste of coconut with vegetables, and find its flavor hard to detect in baked goods. In either case, it may be replaced with a different fat of your choice (olive oil, butter, ghee), though results may vary.

COCONUT SUGAR

Coconut sugar comes from the sap of coconut blossoms and is high in potassium, zinc, magnesium, and iron. It is best known for being lower on the glycemic index than other sugars. What's more, unlike agave nectar, which is high in fructose and often highly processed, it is mostly sucrose, a fructose-glucose combination.

Used in baked goods, coconut sugar imparts a slight caramel flavor and a light brown hue. If you prefer a different option, swap in Sucanat (unrefined cane sugar) or traditional sugar if you like.

GHEE

Ghee is also known as clarified butter—essentially, straight butter oil with all the milk solids removed. The purest ghee is actually casein free and lactose free so it is typically safe for those with milk allergies. Ghee is excellent in baked goods or for high temperature cooking as it has a high smoke point due to the milk solids being removed (which normally would cause butter to burn). Ghee that comes from pastured cows is rich in fat-soluble vitamins A, D, and K.

KEFIR

Kefir is a fermented milk drink made from culturing milk with kefir grains. Featuring a tart flavor and slight effervescence, it has the consistency of a drinkable yogurt. We often use kefir when soaking dough such as in our pizza crust recipe (page 130), as it helps make the final product more digestible. A good replacement for kefir would be organic, full-fat yogurt; just note that results may vary.

MAPLE SYRUP

When we use maple syrup, we're using what is sometimes called Grade B organic maple syrup and other times, Grade A Dark/Robust Taste. Whatever maple syrup you use is generally fine, just make sure it's the real thing and not imitation.

KITCHEN TOOLS

MILK

In our kitchen, we use raw goat's milk, straight from our farmer in Tennessee. Local raw cow's milk or pasteurized whole cow's milk can also be used in our recipes, depending on what works best for your family, or you can swap in whatever type of dairy milk you prefer. Using alternative milks such as almond or coconut is another option, but note that results may vary.

SUCANAT

Sucanat stands for sugar cane natural (su-can-nat) and is unrefined cane sugar (i.e., sugar with its minerals still intact). It is an easy one-to-one swap for coconut sugar or traditional sugar if you like. Its taste is reminiscent of molasses, though a little more muted than that of coconut sugar.

SORGHUM SYRUP (OR SORGHUM MOLASSES)

Made from the sorghum plant, sorghum syrup (also known as sorghum molasses) is a natural sweetener created by processing sorghum juice. Thinner and more tart than molasses, it is rich in phosphorous, magnesium, thiamin, and omega 6 fatty acids. Primarily available in the American South, it is also available online. We like it over pancakes or in cookies, such as our Rosewater Sorghum Shortbread Cookies with Chocolate Drizzle on page 154. If you can't find sorghum syrup, substitute maple syrup instead.

YOGURT

When we use yogurt in a recipe, we are always using full-fat organic yogurt. You may substitute with the yogurt of your choice, but results may vary.

The right tools make any task easier—and that's as true in the kitchen as it is anywhere else. Below are the key kitchen tools you'll see used and highlighted in our recipes, along with reasons for why we like them.

DOUGH SCRAPER

When you mix or knead dough on your counter, the sticky dough will often stick to the counter like glue, making it both hard to work with and hard to clean. That's why a dough scraper becomes your best friend. It easily gets beneath sticky dough and makes it easier to wipe up your mess, and counter.

FOOD PROCESSOR

Our food processor is one of our most invaluable kitchen tools. From puréeing pesto to quickly forming pasta dough, it simplifies cooking and speeds up kitchen work.

GRAIN MILL

A grain mill makes it possible to grind einkorn berries (and other grains) right in your own home, creating flour that is fresh and whole. By grinding the berries fresh for each use, you can ensure that you are getting all the bran, germ, and endosperm from the grain and all the nutrients they contain, including the delicate natural oils. Unlike whole-grain flours that sit on store shelves and risk going rancid due to this exposure, home-ground flour is the most nutritious product possible.

PASTRY CUTTER

We always use a pastry cutter to cut butter into flour, whether it's in a pie crust or a pastry dough. Made of narrow metal strips or wires affixed to a handle, this tool shortens and simplifies the dough-making process.

LET'S GET STARTED!

PIZZA STONE

A good pizza stone is useful for more than baking pizza—we also use ours to bake sourdough bread (page 66) and pitas (page 59), for example. Thanks to its ability to heat up with the oven and create a wider surface area on which foods can bake, a pizza stone helps give bread and other baked goods a strong, crisp crust.

VITAMIX

One of the most respected high-powered blenders on the market, the Vitamix is in constant use in our kitchen. And there's more to this blending tool than morning smoothies—in this book, we use ours for everything from creating unrefined powdered sugar to creating an oatmeal-like consistency in Cream of Einkorn (page 41).

We know that cooking with a new grain can be daunting, but the good news is, it won't feel that way for long. All that's necessary to increase your comfort with einkorn is, as with any other new thing, the willingness to try it out. Once you do, you'll learn quickly that einkorn is truly unique in its structure, nutrient density, texture, and quality. What's more, in cooking, it can be very forgiving—lending itself toward easy adaptations and preferences. That's one of the reasons we put together this book. Let us see you through the introductory phase of using einkorn, and we're confident you'll see what we have: Einkorn offers a rich heritage and a lot of possibilities. So grab your apron and have fun!

CHAPTER 2

Breakfasts

Just like there are mornings to make homemade pancakes and there are mornings to toast the English muffins you baked days before, so there are days filled with rushing and days filled with time to sit and think. We see this variety in our days as grace. That we are given daily opportunities to begin afresh, to start anew—and that those opportunities are seldom exactly alike—demonstrates one of the sweetest gifts we're given in this life: possibility.

❖ Whole-Grain Overnight Pancakes 20

❖ Crisp and Buttery Belgian Waffles 22

❖ Decadent Chocolate Chip Belgian Waffles 23

❖ Cinnamon Doughnut Holes 24

❖ Cinnamon Buns 26

❖ Vanilla Cardamom Breakfast Tea Cake 27

❖ Sourdough English Muffins.... 29

❖ Pear Cinnamon Roll Muffins..30

❖ Cranberry Orange Whole-Grain Muffins 31

❖ Honey Currant Scones 32

❖ Ricotta Vegetable Quiche 35

❖ Potato Rosemary Dutch Baby Pancake with Roasted Red Pepper Sauce 36

❖ Popped Einkorn Berry Parfaits 39

❖ Streusely Banana Bread 40

❖ Cream of Einkorn,................... 41

❖ Apple Pie Breakfast Risotto 42

WHOLE-GRAIN OVERNIGHT PANCAKES

It took some trial and error to come up with these whole-grain einkorn pancakes, which we can now say with confidence turn out perfectly every time—fluffy and light, each one as big as a plate. We like using freshly ground einkorn flour here (although you could certainly swap in a packaged version) because pancakes particularly showcase freshly ground einkorn's natural nutty flavor and light crumb.

* Combine flour, sugar, baking soda, and salt in a large bowl. In a separate bowl, combine 3 tablespoons (42 g) melted butter with eggs, vanilla, kefir, and milk; mix well. Add wet ingredients to dry and stir until all incorporated. Cover and refrigerate overnight.

* In the morning, pull the pancake batter out of the fridge and give it a good stir. If you prefer thinner pancakes, add a little more milk to get the consistency you like. Heat remaining oil or butter in a large skillet and once it's hot, ladle batter into the pan. When bubbles form on the top, flip the pancakes to cook the other side. Finished pancakes may be placed in a warm oven (i.e., your oven's lowest setting) while cooking the rest.

* Top with real maple syrup, butter, fruit, or whatever topping you like best.

Yield: 12 to 15 large pancakes

2 cups (220 g) whole, freshly ground einkorn flour

1 tablespoon (13 g) coconut sugar or Sucanat

1 teaspoon baking soda

1 teaspoon sea salt

4 tablespoons (57 g) butter or coconut oil, melted, divided

3 pastured eggs

1 teaspoon vanilla

¼ cup (60 ml) kefir or yogurt

1 cup (235 ml) whole milk

Toppings, as desired

CRISP AND BUTTERY BELGIAN WAFFLES

These are not your typical Belgian waffles—their exteriors are browned and crisp, but the interiors are light and delicate. I eat them and imagine I'm in a European cafe waiting for a latte. Serve them any way you like, whether that means with syrup and fruit…or with ice cream and hot fudge.

* Preheat your Belgian waffle iron. (We use a 7.5-inch [19 cm] one.)

* In a medium bowl, blend together the egg, vanilla, milk, and melted butter until combined.

* In a separate medium bowl, combine the flour, baking powder, baking soda, salt, and cinnamon; add this dry mixture into the milk mixture, and stir together.

* Spoon about a half a cup (120 ml) of batter at a time onto the hot waffle iron, close, and cook until golden brown.

* Serve with your choice of toppings, such as fruit, syrup, or butter.

Yield: Four 7.5-inch (19 cm) waffles

1 egg

1 teaspoon vanilla extract

1 cup (235 ml) milk

¼ cup (55 g) butter, melted

1 cup (125 g) all-purpose einkorn flour

1 teaspoon baking powder

1 teaspoon baking soda

½ teaspoon sea salt

1 teaspoon cinnamon

Toppings, as desired

DECADENT CHOCOLATE CHIP BELGIAN WAFFLES

Cakey and riddled with chocolate, these waffles are the definition of dessert for breakfast, particularly when topped by fruit, maple syrup, and a little whipped cream. As an added bonus, they're easy to pull together quickly for weekday or weekend mornings alike—we like to eat them on mornings when we need a little comfort food.

* Preheat your Belgian waffle iron. (We use a 7.5-inch [19 cm] one.)

* In a medium bowl, blend together the egg yolks, vanilla, kefir, milk, and melted butter. In a separate bowl, combine the flour, cocoa powder, baking powder, baking soda, sugar, salt, and cinnamon; add this dry mixture into the butter/milk mixture. Add the chopped chocolate and stir everything together until combined.

* Spoon about a half a cup (120 ml) of batter at a time onto the hot waffle iron, close, and cook until golden brown. Repeat with remaining batter until done.

* Serve waffles hot, topped with berries, syrup, butter, or the toppings of your choice.

Yield: Four 7.5-inch (19 cm) Belgian waffles

2 egg yolks

1 teaspoon vanilla extract

¼ cup (60 ml) kefir

¾ cup (175 ml) milk

¼ cup (55 g) butter, melted

1 cup (125 g) all-purpose einkorn flour

1 tablespoon (5 g) cocoa powder

1½ teaspoons baking powder

½ teaspoon baking soda

1½ teaspoons coconut sugar

¼ teaspoon salt

Dash of ground cinnamon

3 ounces (85 g) dark chocolate (preferably at least 70 percent), chopped

Toppings, as desired

CINNAMON DOUGHNUT HOLES

Let's face it, you don't need us to tell you doughnuts are awesome—everybody knows it's hard to beat fried dough rolled in cinnamon and sugar. This einkorn version is especially mouthwatering, formed and rolled at home, dipped into hot oil, and smothered in cinnamon sweetness that sticks to your fingers.

* Combine warm water, ginger powder, yeast, and coconut sugar in a large bowl, and let sit until frothy and bubbly, about 5 to 10 minutes.

* Add 2 cups (200 g) flour, stirring and then mixing with your hands to form it into a sticky ball. Sprinkle remaining ½ cup (50 g) of flour on a counter and lay the ball on top. Work and knead the ball, incorporating most of the flour as you do, for about 5 minutes. The dough is ready once you can form it into a ball that no longer sticks to your hands (any remaining flour on the counter may be saved for the next step, after the dough has risen). Place in an oiled bowl, cover, and let rise for 2 hours, or until doubled in size.

* Once the dough has risen, punch down lightly and divide into 24 small, 1-inch (2.5 cm) balls. Place the balls on a floured piece of parchment to rest for 1 hour, or until lightly risen and around 1½ inches (3.75 cm) in diameter.

* Once the dough is ready, combine sugar and cinnamon on a rimmed plate or wide bowl and set aside. In a small saucepan over medium heat, heat ¾ cup coconut oil (or enough to make 2½ to 3 inches [6.3 to 7.6 cm] deep) until hot, about 350 to 375°F [180 to 190°C].

* Drop 3 or 4 balls of dough into the heated oil, cooking each batch for 2 to 3 minutes, until firm and deep golden. Use a slotted spoon or tongs to remove the doughnuts, transferring to the cinnamon sugar mixture and tossing to coat.

* Set on a paper towel–lined plate and eat immediately. Store leftover doughnuts in a covered container; they'll last a few days.

Yield: 24 doughnut holes

FOR THE DOUGHNUT HOLES:

½ cup (120 ml) warm water (105 to 110°F [40 to 43°C])

1 teaspoon ginger powder

1 packet (2¼ teaspoons, or 9g) active dry yeast

2 tablespoons (26 g) coconut sugar or other sugar

2½ cups (250 g) sifted, whole-grain einkorn flour, divided

Olive oil, for oiling the bowl

¾ cup (175 ml) coconut oil

FOR CINNAMON SUGAR TOPPING:

½ cup (80 g) coconut sugar or other sugar

2 teaspoons cinnamon powder

CINNAMON BUNS

These sweet little einkorn buns came to our kitchen by accident. Working on a different recipe, I'd proofed an extra bowl of yeast on the counter, and Tim said, "Let's try an experiment." What resulted were these pale yellow pillows of dough, which we ensconced in butter and a cinnamon-sugar mix. Small rolls covered in sweetness, they are the exact definition of cinnamon buns.

* In a large bowl, mix together warm water, ginger powder, and honey. Sprinkle yeast on top and stir together. Let sit until frothy and bubbly, about 5 to 10 minutes.

* Once yeast mixture is frothy, add salt and yogurt, stirring to combine. Add einkorn flour, ½ cup at a time, mixing dough together with a spoon until it starts to come together. Use clean, floured hands to knead together until you get a smooth, workable dough. Form it into a ball and let it rest in the bowl, covered, for 1 hour.

* Line 2 baking sheets with parchment paper. Place the melted ghee or butter in 1 small bowl. In another small bowl, combine cinnamon and sugar.

* Turn the dough out onto a floured surface. If it sticks to your hands, add a bit more flour (up to ½ cup [63 g]) to make it easier to handle. Form dough into 20 to 30 small balls.

* Brush or roll balls in melted ghee, then in the cinnamon-sugar mixture. Place the balls on prepared baking sheets and let rest in a warm place for another 30 to 45 minutes; buns should spread slightly, causing cracks in the cinnamon sugar mixture.

* Preheat oven to 400°F (200°C, or gas mark 6). Bake buns for 10 minutes, until puffy and slightly golden.

Yield: 20 to 30 buns

¾ cup (175 ml) warm water (105 to 110°F [40 to 43°C])

⅛ teaspoon ginger powder

2 tablespoons (40 g) honey

1 packet (2¼ teaspoons [9 g]) active dry yeast

¼ teaspoon sea salt

1 tablespoon (15 g) yogurt

2¼ cups (281 g) all-purpose einkorn flour, plus up to another ½ cup (63 g) for forming the dough

2 tablespoons (28 g) melted ghee or butter

2 teaspoons cinnamon

¼ cup (40 g) coconut sugar or Sucanat

Recipe Note

• *If you're in a rush, skip the second rise for these buns; they'll rise a little less and be a touch smaller, but they'll still be addictively good.*

VANILLA CARDAMOM BREAKFAST TEA CAKE

This dreamy breakfast dessert cake incorporates a whopping 3 or 4 vanilla beans into the batter, but don't let that deter you from trying it out. For one thing, it's not hard to find vanilla beans for good prices online, but, besides that, their potent flavor is irreplaceable here. Paired with the cardamom and sweet, black tea icing, this cake is quite a standout. When we make it, we can't stop sneaking slices.

∗ Preheat oven to 350°F (180°C, or gas mark 4) and grease an 8.5 x 4.5-inch (22 x 12 cm) loaf pan.

∗ In a small bowl, combine flour, baking powder, sea salt, cardamom, and nutmeg. In a separate bowl, beat together butter, eggs, milk, vanilla scraped out of vanilla bean pods (x2) (reserve the sucanet), and vanilla extract, until creamy and well incorporated. Slowly add dry ingredients to the wet ingredients and mix just until all the flour is incorporated.

∗ Pour batter into prepared pan and bake for 50 to 60 minutes, or until a toothpick comes out clean. Let cool until you are able to remove the loaf from the pan, about 5 to 10 minutes, and place on a wire rack.

∗ To make the glaze, boil the water with leftover vanilla bean pods for 5 minutes. Add the tea bag and steep for 3 to 5 minutes. In a small bowl or measuring cup (it helps to have a pour spout) combine the powdered Sucanat with about 3 tablespoons (45 ml) of the vanilla black tea (drink the remainder or reserve it in the fridge for another use). Let glaze cool until it's thickened slightly, then pour over cake. Cool until icing is firm. Slice to serve.

Yield: 1 loaf, or 12 to 15 slices

FOR THE CAKE:

2 cups (250 g) all-purpose einkorn flour

1 teaspoon baking powder

¼ teaspoon sea salt

¼ teaspoon cardamom

¹⁄₁₆ teaspoon nutmeg

3 tablespoons (42 g) butter or coconut oil, softened

⅔ cup (67 g) Sucanat

2 eggs

½ cup (120 ml) milk

3 large or 4 small vanilla bean pods, scraped, with pods reserved for glaze

1 teaspoon vanilla extract

FOR THE GLAZE:

1 cup (240 ml) water

3 to 4 vanilla bean pods (leftover from cake ingredients)

1 black tea bag

½ cup (80 g) powdered Sucanat

SOURDOUGH ENGLISH MUFFINS

Whether you top these English muffins with butter and jam or with eggs and turkey bacon, we hope you toast them before you do. If you ask us, there's no better way to eat a homemade English muffin than straight out of the toaster, crisp and warmed.

* At least 8 hours ahead of time, stir together initial dough ingredients in a large bowl. Cover with a towel and let rest at room temperature overnight or for 8 hours.

* After the rest period is over, add the final dough ingredients, beginning with ½ cup (63 g) flour, and stir together. Turn this mixture out onto a floured work surface and knead for 5 to 10 minutes. The dough will be soft and sticky, but add as little extra flour as possible in order to keep working with it.

* After kneading, separate dough into 8 equal portions. With floured fingers, shape these portions into balls and place them on flour-dusted parchment paper. Cover the balls for 45 minutes to an hour.

* After resting, warm a large cast iron skillet over medium-low heat and brush with coconut oil. Once pan is hot, cook muffins for 5 to 10 minutes on each side, flipping frequently in the first few minutes.

* Cool on a wire rack and split open with a fork to serve.

Yield: 8 English muffins

FOR THE INITIAL DOUGH:

½ cup (110 g) sourdough starter

½ cup (120 ml) whole milk

½ cup (120 ml) water

⅔ to 1 cup (83 to 125 g) all-purpose einkorn flour, depending on starter's hydration

FOR THE FINAL DOUGH:

½ to 1 cup (63 to 125 g) all-purpose einkorn flour, plus more for surfaces

2 tablespoons (26 g) sugar

1 teaspoon sea salt

1 teaspoon baking soda

½ tablespoon (6 g) coconut oil, melted, for brushing

PEAR CINNAMON ROLL MUFFINS

*W*e call these pear cinnamon roll muffins because, fresh from the oven, they look beautifully dark and swirled, with a sticky filling reminiscent of those lip-smacking bakery treats.

* Preheat oven to 375°F (190°C, or gas mark 5) and line a 12-cup muffin pan with paper liners. Fill a baking sheet with hazelnuts and toast in the oven for about 10 minutes, until fragrant and dark. Remove and let nuts cool slightly.

* Meanwhile, in a small saucepan over medium heat, combine pears, maple syrup, cinnamon, nutmeg, salt, and butter. Cook, uncovered, for about 10 minutes, stirring often, and mashing with a fork as things soften. Lower heat to a simmer; add apple cider vinegar. Let mixture keep reducing while you make the muffin batter, about 20 minutes, until reduced to ¾ cup (175 ml).

* Rub cooled hazelnuts between your fingers to shake off skins, if desired, and grind them in a food processor until tiny, like very coarse sand. Combine nuts with flour, baking powder, salt, and sugar in a medium bowl. In a separate bowl, whisk 1 egg; stir in milk and vanilla.

* Stir wet mixture into the dry one. Divide batter evenly among muffin cups and spoon pear compote evenly among them. Stir together cinnamon and sugar in a small bowl and sprinkle on top of muffin cups.

* Bake for 20 to 25 minutes, until brown on top and a toothpick inserted in the center comes out clean. Serve warm. Leftover muffins keep for up to a week, refrigerated in an airtight container.

Yield: 12 muffins

FOR THE TOASTED NUTS:

½ cup (70 g) shelled hazelnuts

FOR THE PEAR COMPOTE:

2 ripe pears, peeled, cored, and chopped

¼ cup (60 ml) maple syrup

½ teaspoon ground cinnamon

½ teaspoon ground nutmeg

¼ teaspoon sea salt

1 tablespoon (14 g) butter

1 teaspoon apple cider vinegar

FOR THE MUFFIN BATTER:

2 cups (250 g) all-purpose einkorn flour

1 tablespoon (14 g) baking powder

½ teaspoon sea salt

¼ cup (40 g) coconut sugar

1 egg

1 cup (235 ml) whole milk or kefir

2 teaspoons vanilla extract

½ tablespoon (7 g) sugar

½ tablespoon (3 g) ground cinnamon

Recipe Note

• *Because this muffin batter doesn't call for butter or oil, it's important to use full-fat milk or kefir here.*

CRANBERRY ORANGE WHOLE-GRAIN MUFFINS

*Yield: 10 large
bakery-style muffins*

Sparkling with orange sugar and beautifully puffed, these orange cranberry muffins could rival any bakery's. What's more, the whole-grain texture of the batter is the perfect complement to the sweetened cranberries inside.

* Preheat oven to 350°F (180°C, or gas mark 4).

* In a saucepan over medium low heat, add cranberries, half the orange zest, orange juice, and coconut sugar. Cook for 5 to 10 minutes, until dark and wilted, almost like a cranberry sauce. Remove from heat and set aside to cool.

* In a large bowl, combine flour, coconut sugar, baking powder, and sea salt. Add melted butter and milk and stir; the batter should be thick and not runny. Fold in cranberry mixture until well incorporated. Fill muffin cups almost to the top, or for even larger muffins, use lotus parchment cups and fill to the ledge.

* Combine coarse sugar with remaining orange zest in a small bowl and mix together. Sprinkle orange-sugar on top of each muffin.

* Bake for 22 minutes or until a toothpick inserted in the centres comes out clean.

FOR THE CRANBERRIES:

2 cups (176 g) fresh cranberries, halved

2 tablespoons (12 g) orange zest (from about 2 oranges), divided

¼ cup (60 ml) orange juice

¼ cup (40 g) coconut sugar or Sucanat

FOR THE MUFFIN BATTER:

2½ cups (275 g) whole-grain flour

⅔ cup (106 g) coconut sugar or Sucanat

1 tablespoon (14 g) baking powder

½ teaspoon sea salt

6 tablespoons (85 g) butter, melted

1 cup (235 ml) whole milk

2 tablespoons (26 g) coarse sugar, for sprinkling on top

HONEY CURRANT SCONES

Currants complement the sweet nature of this scone dough, which bakes beautifully into golden wedges. Flaky, buttery, and just a little more moist than traditional scones, these scones are highly addictive, so consider yourself warned—once you have one, it's hard to stop.

* Preheat oven to 375°F (190°C, or gas mark 5) and line a baking sheet with parchment paper.

* In a large bowl, combine flour, baking powder, and salt. Cut in cubed butter with a pastry cutter or 2 forks until the mixture looks like coarse crumbs. Then stir in honey and milk until a sticky dough is formed. Stir in currants last, which will give the dough more structure. Turn the dough out on a floured surface.

* Form the dough into a ball and flatten into a 6- to 7-inch (15 to 18 cm) round (depending on the thickness you prefer). Transfer to prepared baking sheet using a dough scraper. Cut into 6 equal wedges and if desired brush the top thinly with yogurt (or egg wash).

* Bake for 15 to 18 minutes, until golden. Serve warm or cool, alongside a hot cup of tea.

Yield: 6 scones

FOR THE SCONES:

2½ cups (281 g) all-purpose einkorn flour

1½ tablespoons (21 g) baking powder

½ teaspoon sea salt

6 tablespoons (85 g) butter, chilled and cubed into half tablespoons (7 g)

⅓ cup (115 g) honey

½ cup (120 ml) whole milk

⅔ cup (100 g) currants

FOR THE EGG WASH:

1 to 2 tablespoons (15 to 30 g) whole-milk yogurt (or 1 egg, beaten with a teaspoon of water)

RICOTTA VEGETABLE QUICHE

To us, a ricotta vegetable quiche is classic brunch food—refined and elegant while also hearty and filling, perfect for pairing with leafy greens and fruit. This recipe combines our buttery, flaky einkorn crust with a vegetable-laden egg filling lightened with ricotta cheese.

﹡ Preheat oven to 375°F (190°C, or gas mark 5). Warm coconut oil in a 9-inch (23 cm) skillet over medium-low heat. Stir in chopped bell pepper, chopped onion, chopped mushrooms, and chopped tomatoes, and sauté until soft and translucent, but not browned, about 8 to 10 minutes. Remove from heat and let cool slightly.

﹡ In a large bowl, whisk together eggs until combined and slightly frothy. Stir in milk and ricotta until combined.

﹡ Add spinach, red chili flakes, salt, and pepper to vegetable mixture, and stir together until well mixed and the spinach is coated with oil and wilted from the heat. Add this combined vegetable mixture to the egg mixture.

﹡ Remove pie crust dough from the refrigerator to a floured surface. Grease a 9- to 10-inch (23 to 25 cm) pie pan. Use a rolling pin to flatten the dough to be a little larger than the pie pan. Using floured hands, press dough into prepared pan, trimming the edges as you like. Pour vegetable-egg mixture into pan. Place the pan in the oven and bake for 45 minutes to an hour, or until set and slightly golden. You'll know it's done when a knife or toothpick inserted into the center comes out clean. Let cool at least a few minutes, and slice to serve. Serve warm or chilled.

Yield: 6 to 8 servings

1 tablespoon (13 g) coconut oil

1 cup (140 g) chopped bell pepper (from about 1 bell pepper)

½ cup (80 g) chopped onion (from about half an onion)

½ cup (42 g) chopped baby bella/cremini mushrooms

½ cup (80 g) chopped tomatoes

4 eggs

¼ cup (60 ml) whole milk

¾ cup (180 g) ricotta cheese

1 cup (50 g) packed baby spinach

1 teaspoon red chili flakes

¾ teaspoon sea salt

½ teaspoon black pepper

Flaky All-Butter Pie Crust dough (page 156) or Hearty Whole-Grain Pie Crust dough (page 157), chilled

POTATO ROSEMARY DUTCH BABY PANCAKE
WITH ROASTED RED PEPPER SAUCE

*I*f there's anything better than a puffed pancake, it's this savory puffed pancake, studded with potatoes that crisp up like oven fries alongside bits of fresh rosemary. Topped with a cheesy roasted pepper sauce, this show-stopping breakfast is part pancake, part quiche, and part pizza—as refined and elegant as it is grownup comfort food.

* Preheat oven to 450°F (230°C, or gas mark 8). Peel potatoes and slice as thinly as possible with a knife or a mandolin. Place a 10-inch (25 cm) cast iron pan over medium heat and add coconut oil. Add potatoes and rosemary, stirring to coat with oil. Cook for about 5 minutes, until potatoes are soft and slightly golden on the bottom. Move pan from stove to oven, letting it continue cooking for 5 to 10 minutes.

* Meanwhile, in a blender or food processor, combine milk, flour, eggs, butter, Sucanat or coconut sugar, vanilla extract, and salt. Once well mixed, pour this batter into the pan of potatoes in the oven. Continue baking for another 20 to 25 minutes, until golden brown on top and fully set in the middle, enough so that a tooth-pick inserted in the middle comes out clean. While pancake bakes, make red pepper sauce by pureeing roasted peppers, olive oil, and grated Pecorino in a blender or food processor.

* Remove pancake from oven when fully baked and beautifully puffy, top with pepper sauce, and cut into wedges to serve.

Yield: 6 servings

FOR THE PANCAKE:

2 medium (350 g) potatoes

2 tablespoons (26 g) coconut oil

1 tablespoon (2 g) freshly chopped rosemary

¾ cup (175 ml) milk

1 cup (125 g) all-purpose einkorn flour

3 eggs

2 tablespoons (28 g) butter, melted and cooled

2 tablespoons (26 g) Sucanat or coconut sugar

1 teaspoon vanilla extract

½ teaspoon sea salt

FOR THE PEPPER SAUCE:

½ cup (95 g) roasted red pepper slices

½ cup (120 ml) olive oil

¼ cup (25 g) grated Pecorino cheese

POPPED EINKORN BERRY PARFAITS

*W*hen you bake soaked, dehydrated einkorn berries in a high-heat oven, they pop and jump in a way reminiscent of popcorn on the stove. The resulting berries remind us of honey cereals we ate as kids—crunchy, sticky, and sweet—and, in parfaits like this one, they're like an einkorn spin on granola, the ideal finishing touch to yogurt, berries, and honey (and one we'd gladly eat every day).

* At least 4 hours ahead of time and up to the night before, soak einkorn berries in enough water to cover and add a teaspoon of apple cider vinegar. When ready to use, drain, rinse, and dry. There are three ways to dry the berries: Spread them out evenly on a baking sheet and place it in a closed, unheated oven overnight; preheat the oven to its lowest setting, spread berries out on a baking sheet, and bake for 1 to 2 hours, stirring once or twice; or, using a dehydrator, dry berries until dry on the outside.

* Preheat oven to 500°F (260°C, or gas mark 10). (If you've dried the berries in the oven, be sure to remove them before turning the oven on.) Once preheated, add cookie sheet with berries, and bake until popped, about 3 to 5 minutes. They will not pop up significantly in appearance, but you should hear them popping and cracking open. If you let them go too long, they will burn, so keep an eye on them. In a separate bowl, combine melted butter, honey, and sea salt. Toss popped einkorn berries with butter/honey mixture until evenly coated.

* To assemble the parfaits, mix 2 tablespoons (40 g) of honey with yogurt. In 2 separate bowls or glasses, add a layer of yogurt on the bottom, then popped einkorn, then fruit, then another layer of yogurt, then popped einkorn, and so on. Drizzle an additional tablespoon (20 g) of honey on top of each parfait to serve.

Yield: 2 servings

FOR THE BERRIES:

½ cup (100 g) einkorn berries

1 teaspoon apple cider vinegar

2 teaspoons butter, melted

2 teaspoons honey

¼ teaspoon sea salt

FOR THE PARFAITS:

16 ounces (453 g) organic yogurt

¼ cup (85 g) honey, divided

4 ounces (125 g) blueberries

6 ounces (170 g) raspberries

STREUSELY BANANA BREAD

*If you ask us, homemade banana bread is about as comforting as it gets, especially sweet and soft, eaten fresh from the oven. This version is more than its firm crust and delectable crumb almost as soft as pudding, however; it's also easy. By mixing the batter in a food processor rather than a bowl, you skip the typical step of softening butter before mixing; instead, cold butter goes straight into the food processor, and the entire batter is combined there.

✳ Preheat oven to 350°F (180°C, or gas mark 4) and grease an 8.5 x 4.5-inch (22 x 12 cm) loaf pan.

✳ In a small bowl, whisk together dry ingredients (flour, baking soda, salt). Place the butter and sugar in a food processor, and blend until combined, with the mixture pulling away from the sides and forming into 1 giant slab of dough. Add eggs, one at a time, blending until absorbed. Add mashed bananas, yogurt, and vanilla, and blend until combined. Add dry ingredients, and blend until combined again. Pour into prepared loaf pan.

✳ In a small bowl, combine Sucanat and cinnamon for streusel topping, and pour this mixture on top of the loaf. Bake for 50 to 60 minutes, until a knife inserted in the center comes out clean. Serve warm or at room temperature.

Yield: 8 to 10 slices

◇◇◇◇◇◇◇◇◇◇◇◇◇◇◇◇◇◇◇◇◇◇◇◇◇◇◇

FOR THE BREAD:

1¾ cups (218 g) all-purpose einkorn flour

¾ teaspoon baking soda

½ teaspoon salt

6 tablespoons (85 g) butter, cold and cut into tablespoons (14 g)

¾ cup (120 g) coconut sugar or Sucanat

2 eggs

1 cup (250 g) mashed ripe bananas (from about 2 large)

½ cup (160 g) full-fat plain yogurt

½ teaspoon vanilla

FOR THE STREUSEL-LIKE TOPPING:

¼ cup (40 g) Sucanat

1 tablespoon (7 g) cinnamon

CREAM OF EINKORN

*B*y grinding your own berries, you control the texture of this comforting breakfast bowl: For a super-fine, porridge-like result, grind the berries in a grain mill, or use 1½ cups (165 g) of whole-grain einkorn flour. For a more textured, oatmeal-like consistency, pulse the berries in a food processor or Vitamix until the size of steel-cut oats, as directed below. In either case, prepare to enjoy a hot, creamy bowl of slightly tart, nutty morning comfort that's as perfect for starting a cold winter day as it is for savoring a summer one.

✳ In a medium bowl, combine ground einkorn berries, water, and apple cider vinegar, cover, and soak overnight.

✳ In the morning, pour prepared mixture into a saucepan and cook over medium heat for 10 to 15 minutes, whisking frequently, until as thick as oatmeal, spoonable, and no longer liquidic. Skim off any scum (i.e., white, frothy mixture) that rises to the top with a large spoon. Divide the mixture between 2 bowls and top each with a tablespoon of butter (14 g), 2 teaspoons (6 g) of your preferred sweetener, ¼ cup (38 g) of fruit, and a tablespoon (15 ml) of milk. Serve warm.

Yield: Two 1-cup servings or four ½-cup servings

FOR THE BERRIES:

1 cup (200 g) einkorn berries, roughly ground

2 cups (475 ml) water

1 tablespoon (15 ml) apple cider vinegar

FOR SERVING:

2 tablespoons (28 g) butter

4 teaspoons (11 g) Sucanat, honey, or maple syrup

½ cup (77 g) frozen fruit

2 tablespoons (28 ml) milk

APPLE PIE BREAKFAST RISOTTO

This slow-cooking risotto is something to save for a weekend or slow morning—but, in the middle of cold winter weather, there are few foods more comforting. Hot, sweet, and decadent, this is a stick-to-your-ribs day starter that's irresistible.

* The night before making the risotto, set berries in a small bowl with enough water to cover and the apple cider vinegar. Cover with a towel and let sit at room temperature overnight.

* In the morning, rinse and drain the berries. In a stockpot over medium heat, melt ghee. Lower the heat to medium-low and add cinnamon, nutmeg, ginger, and cardamom, and use a wooden spoon to toss these spices in the ghee, letting them liquefy and coat the pan, about 3 to 5 minutes. Add diced apple, toss to coat, and add einkorn berries, stirring everything together. Let cook 5 minutes, stirring often. Add ½ cup (120 ml) apple juice, raise the heat to medium-high, and stir the mixture as it cooks and simmers. Once the juice has absorbed, so that when you move some of the mixture in the pan, liquids don't immediately refill the space, add another ½ cup (120 ml). Keep repeating this process, adding ½ cup (120 ml) of juice, stirring until it is mostly absorbed, and doing it again, until you have added 3 cups (705 ml) of juice. It should take 45 to 60 minutes. Taste mixture; if the berries are still crunchy, add the remaining ½ cup (120 ml) apple juice and keep cooking. When ready, the berries should be no longer hard, but instead al dente.

* Meanwhile, set a skillet on another burner over medium heat, and toast pecans for 5 to 7 minutes, until fragrant but not burned. Remove from heat and let cool slightly. Toward the end of cook time, move pecans to a cutting board and chop roughly.

* Once risotto is cooked and liquids are absorbed, remove from heat. Stir in ricotta and toasted pecans. Serve immediately; garnish with extra cinnamon and milk, if desired.

Yield: 2 servings

½ cup (100 g) einkorn berries

1 teaspoon apple cider vinegar

1 tablespoon (14 g) ghee

1 tablespoon (7 g) cinnamon

1 teaspoon nutmeg

1 teaspoon ginger powder

¼ teaspoon cardamom

1 large (228 g) apple, peeled and diced into ½- to 1-inch (13 mm to 2.5 cm) chunks

3 to 3½ cups (705 to 823 ml) pure apple juice

½ cup (55 g) pecans

¼ cup (65 g) ricotta

¼ cup (60 ml) whole milk

CHAPTER 3

When it comes to einkorn, bread is a beautiful way to make this ancient grain shine. From yeasty cinnamon raisin bread to a quick batch of pitas, einkorn breads and doughs are some of the clearest showcases of the delicious forms einkorn can take. With all-purpose einkorn flour, expect a pale yellow hue and slighty nutty flavor; with whole-grain einkorn flour, expect a hearty, grainy texture. In either case, einkorn bread offers that same addictive quality all lifelong bread-lovers understand.

❖ Soft Sandwich Loaf 45
❖ One-Bowl Butter Bread 46
❖ Marble Rye Bread 49
❖ Cinnamon Raisin Bread 50
❖ Spinach Skillet Cornbread 52
❖ Dinner Rolls 54
❖ Whole-Grain Dinner Rolls 55
❖ Focaccia with Caramelized Onions and Tomatoes 56

❖ Rosemary Breadsticks 57
❖ Soft, Pillowy Pita Pockets 59
❖ Simple Homemade Tortillas 60
❖ Avocado Parathas 62
❖ Sourdough Slider Buns 63
❖ Pretzel Rolls 65
❖ Classic Artisan Sourdough Bread 66

❖ Cherry Walnut Sourdough Boule 68
❖ Whole-Grain Sourdough 68
❖ Garlic Cheese Sourdough Croutons 70
❖ Herbed Bread Crumbs 70

SOFT SANDWICH LOAF

*A*s soon as we started using einkorn flour, we knew we wanted to make a simple einkorn sandwich loaf, one that would be a go-to for sandwiches, toast, and more. What we love about this version is that it is not only those things, but, thanks to the added butter and coconut oil, it is also one of the softest, lightest breads either of us has ever had. That full tablespoon (18 g) of salt does more than bring out the nutty einkorn flour, too: It also protects against overproofing and helps the soft bread hold its shape. Use this recipe for a classic peanut butter and jelly sandwich, and prepare to fall in love.

* Combine ¼ cup (60 ml) of warm water, yeast, and 1 tablespoon (21 g) of honey in a large bowl; let sit for 5 to 10 minutes in a warm place, until bubbly and frothy. If mixture does not bubble and froth, wait longer or start over. This step is crucial.

* Add remaining tablespoon (21 g) of honey, milk, remaining ¼ cup (60 ml) of water, coconut oil, butter, and salt; stir together. Add 1 cup (125 g) of flour at a time, stirring after each addition, until you can use your hands to form a ball of dough (note: wetter dough = softer loaf) and place it in an oiled bowl. Cover and let sit for 30 minutes. Then, dust the dough and a work surface with flour, and knead dough for 5 to 10 minutes, adding more flour as needed, until dough is smooth and elastic. Reform into a ball, place back in the oiled bowl, cover with a towel, and let rest for 45 minutes in a warm place. Form into loaf and place in a greased 8.5 x 4.5-inch (22 x 12 cm) loaf pan. Cover with plastic wrap and let rest for 1 to 2 hours, until it's puffed out a little and filled the pan.

* Toward the end of the rise period, preheat oven to 375°F (190°C, or gas mark 5).

* Once ready, slash the top of the loaf vertically down the middle, brush it with milk, and bake for 30 to 45 minutes, until browned. (The bottom should also sound hollow when tapped.)

Yield: One loaf

- ½ cup (120 ml) warm water (105 to 110°F [40 to 43°C]), divided
- 1 packet (2¼ teaspoons, or 9 g) active dry yeast
- 2 tablespoons (42 g) honey, divided
- ½ cup (120 ml) milk
- 1 tablespoon (13 g) coconut oil, melted
- 1 tablespoon (14 g) butter, melted
- 1 tablespoon (18 g) sea salt
- 3 to 3½ cups (375 to 438 g) all-purpose einkorn flour, plus more for dusting fingers and work surface
- 1 to 2 teaspoons (125 g) milk, for brushing loaf before baking

Recipe Note

For a whole-grain twist on the soft sandwich bread, swap in the same weight (3¾ to 4⅓ cups, or 375 to 438 g) of whole-grain einkorn flour for the all-purpose. What will result is a heartier, grainer version of the sandwich bread, one that is denser but just as delicious.

ONE-BOWL BUTTER BREAD

Yield: 1 loaf

𝒯im is an idea guy (we once spent an entire 2-hour date in a cafe, drumming up 100 possible future businesses, him smiling ear to ear). So it's no surprise that sometimes he'll announce a recipe he wants to try, designed strictly in his head—and that's the way this bowl bread came to be. Looking for a basic bread recipe that could both come together, rise, and bake in the same container, he came up with this simple version of a hearty, soft loaf that slices up beautifully for crostini like the ones on page 77. With a crisp crust and a soft crumb, this one-bowl bread is enough to make idea lovers out of all of us.

1 packet (2¼ teaspoons, or 9 g) active dry yeast

1 teaspoon sugar

1 cup (235 ml) warm water (105 to 110°F [40 to 43°C])

3 cups (375 g) all-purpose einkorn flour

1 teaspoon sea salt

3 tablespoons (42 g) butter melted, divided, for brushing dough and bowl

✳ In a large bowl, combine yeast with sugar and warm water, and let sit for 5 to 10 minutes, until frothy and bubbly. Add flour and salt to yeast mixture, stir together until it begins to come together, and then use your clean, floured hands to form it into a dough. Turn dough out onto floured surface and knead for a minute or two, until smooth. Let rest on the counter for 10 minutes. In the meantime, butter the inside of an oven-safe 1- or 2-quart bowl (such as Pyrex). Knead dough for another 1 to 2 minutes; add to the buttered bowl, cover with a towel, and let rise for 2 hours in a warm place.

✳ After dough has risen, preheat oven to 375°F (190°C, or gas mark 5). Gently brush the top of the dough with the remainder of melted butter, and place the oven-safe bowl with dough in the oven. Bake for 35 minutes, until golden on top and hollow when tapped. Invert the bowl and let the bread cool on a rack or cutting board. Crust should be golden and crisp with a soft inside. Once cooled, slice bread to use for sandwiches, toast, or crostini (see headnote).

MARBLE RYE BREAD

We love this marbled einkorn rye both because of its traditional rye flavor and because of its beautifully swirled insides. It's especially nice on BLTs (page 112), or toasted and covered in jam.

* Prepare Dough 1: Proof yeast by whisking it with warm water and honey in a bowl and letting sit 10 minutes or longer, until frothy and bubbly. If yeast hasn't activated in that time, let it rest longer or start over. Don't skip this; if the yeast shows no activity, it is likely dead, and your bread won't rise. Add einkorn flour, rye flour, salt, caraway seeds, and milk. Knead briefly, about 1 to 2 minutes, until dough comes together. Form into a ball of dough and let rest, covered, for 30 minutes right in bowl.

* Prepare Dough 2: Repeat the process above for dough 1 but with dough 2 ingredients.

* After doughs have rested, preheat oven to 375°F (190°C, or gas mark 5) and grease a 9 x 5-inch or 8 x 4-inch (23 x 13 cm or 20 x 10 cm) loaf pan. Divide each dough into 3 equal portions. Roll out each portion to approximately 9 x 4 inches, or a little larger than the pan you are using. Once all 6 portions are rolled out, you can stack them, twist them, braid them, or roll them together. For the stacking method, stack them on top of each other while alternating the doughs: light, dark, light, dark, and so on. Curl the sides down and under the stack and place in the loaf pan. Cover and let rise for 60 to 90 minutes, until doubled in size.

* Brush with egg wash. Bake for 35 to 40 minutes, until loaf sounds hollow when tapped.

Yield: 1 loaf, or 14 to 16 slices

FOR DOUGH 1:

1 packet (2¼ teaspoons [9 g]) active dry yeast

¼ cup (60 ml) warm water (105 to 115°F [40 to 46°C])

1 teaspoon honey or sugar

1¼ cup (156 g) all-purpose einkorn flour, plus extra for dusting

⅔ cup (75 g) whole-grain rye flour

½ teaspoon sea salt

2 teaspoons caraway seeds

½ cup (120 ml) milk

FOR DOUGH 2:

1 packet (2¼ teaspoons [9 g]) active dry yeast

¼ cup (60 ml) warm water (100 to 110°F [37 to 43°C])

1 teaspoon honey or sugar

1¼ cups (156 g) all-purpose einkorn flour, plus up to 1 cup (125 g)

⅔ cup (75 g) rye flour

2 tablespoons (11 g) cocoa powder

3 tablespoons (60 g) molasses

½ teaspoon sea salt

1 teaspoon caraway seeds

½ cup (120 ml) milk

FOR THE EGG WASH:

1 egg, beaten

CINNAMON RAISIN BREAD

When I was a little girl, sleeping over at my grandma's house, she showed me her favorite late-night snack: toasted cinnamon raisin bread with sliced apples on the side. When we make this einkorn version, with its light crumb and pale golden hue, I eat a toasted slice, I think of her, and it's as if I'm 6 years old again. Even without the memories though, this bread is a showstopper: dark and domed on the outside, perfectly swirled in the interior.

* In a saucepan over medium heat, stir together butter, milk, kefir, coconut sugar, and salt. Bring to the beginning of a boil (where a few little bubbles start coming up on the surface); remove from heat and set aside to cool.

* Proof yeast by whisking it with warm water, ginger powder, and honey in a large bowl and letting sit 10 minutes or longer, until frothy and bubbly. If yeast hasn't activated in that time, let it rest longer or start over. Don't skip this; if the yeast shows no activity, it is likely dead, and your bread won't rise. Combine filling ingredients in a small bowl.

* Add cooled milk mixture to the yeast mixture, and whisk in 1 egg. Stir in 2 cups (250 g) of the einkorn flour with a wooden spoon. Keep adding more flour until the batter begins to feel stiff and comes together, no longer sticky and able to be formed into a ball.

* Lightly flour your work surface, then turn out dough and knead for 5 to 8 minutes, working to develop an elastic, soft texture in the dough. Form it into a ball and place in a greased bowl, turning once to coat. Cover and let rise until doubled in size, about an hour.

* After dough has doubled, punch it down. On a floured surface, roll the dough out into a rectangle 16 inches (41 cm) wide and 9 inches (23 cm) long. Spread the filling mixture evenly all over the dough, leaving a ¼-inch to ½-inch (3 mm to 6 mm) border along the edges. Starting at the shorter end, roll the dough up like a jelly roll. Tuck the ends under each side and place the dough in a greased 8.5 x 4.5-inch (22 x 12 cm) loaf pan. Cover and let rise for 45 minutes to an hour; it should rise and puff out to fill the pan.

Yield: 1 loaf, about 15 slices

FOR THE BREAD:

6 tablespoons (85 g) unsalted butter, plus more for brushing

½ cup (120 ml) milk

¼ cup (60 ml) kefir

¼ cup (40 g) coconut sugar

1 teaspoon sea salt

1 packet (2¼ teaspoons [9 g]) active dry yeast

¼ cup (60 ml) warm water (105 to 115°F [40 to 46°C])

1 teaspoon ginger powder

1 tablespoon honey

2 eggs, divided

Up to 4 cups (500 g) all-purpose einkorn flour, plus more for dusting

FOR THE FILLING:

¼ cup (40 g) coconut sugar

2 tablespoons (14 g) cinnamon

¼ cup (40 g) raisins

✳ Toward the end of the rise period, preheat oven to 350°F (180°C, or gas mark 4). Once the loaf is ready, beat the remaining egg in a small bowl and brush it all over the top of the loaf. Bake bread for 45 minutes. Transfer to a wire rack, butter the top, and let bread cool completely before removing from pan to serve.

SPINACH SKILLET CORNBREAD

As northerners who now live in Tennessee, cornbread presents something of a controversy. In the South, where we live, cornbread is usually savory, made sans sugar and often cooked in bacon grease; in Illinois and Ohio, where we grew up, cornbread is more of a cake, sweet and delicate, often made in muffin cups. In this spinach skillet version, we combine the best of both worlds. Savory, bacon-infused spinach blends with a sweet, light corn cake and it's hard to stop eating.

One of the most surprising things about this recipe is that, beyond the grease the spinach is cooked in, there is no oil or butter in the mix. True confession: That's because we forgot to add it when we tested the recipe—but, after we tasted this airy, sweet and savory result, we realized we'd stumbled upon a winner.

* Preheat oven to 450°F (230°C, or gas mark 8). Heat bacon grease in a 10-inch (25 cm) cast iron skillet over medium heat. Add 4 cups (125 g) chopped fresh spinach and ½ teaspoon salt. Cook for 5 to 10 minutes, until wilted. Remove from heat.

* While the spinach is cooking, in a large bowl, combine einkorn flour, cornmeal, coconut sugar, baking powder, and salt. In a separate, small bowl, whisk together eggs and combine with honey, yogurt, and water. Add this wet mixture to the dry one. Pour batter over cooked spinach using a spoon to spread the batter evenly over the greens.

* Lower oven temperature to 375°F (190°C, or gas mark 5) and immediately put skillet inside. Bake for 15 to 20 minutes, until a toothpick inserted in the center comes out clean. Cool in pan for 10 minutes, then run a butter knife along the edges and turn the skillet over onto a cutting board or platter. Serve bread warm or cool, with butter on top.

Yield: One 10-inch (25 cm) cornbread, about 8 servings

FOR THE SPINACH:

1 tablespoon (13 g) bacon grease

4 cups (125 g) chopped fresh spinach

½ teaspoon sea salt

FOR THE CORNBREAD:

1½ cups (187 g) all-purpose einkorn flour

¾ cup (105 g) cornmeal

½ cup (80 g) coconut sugar

1 tablespoon (14 g) baking powder

½ teaspoon sea salt

2 eggs, beaten

3 tablespoons (60 g) honey

½ cup (115 g) whole-milk plain yogurt

¼ cup (60 ml) water

DINNER ROLLS

*W*ith a firm, golden crust and a soft, yeasty interior, these dinner rolls are incredibly versatile. We recommend making them alongside a meal with lots of sauce or gravy, using the dinner rolls to sop up flavorful juices.

* In a large bowl, combine warm water and honey, and sprinkle yeast over the top, quickly combining the mixture with a fork. Let yeast mixture sit for 5 to 10 minutes, until frothy and bubbly. If the mixture is not very frothy, give it more time or start over. The yeast must be activated in order for the rolls to rise. Meanwhile, in a medium-size bowl, stir together 2¾ cups (344 g) flour, salt, milk, and 2 tablespoons (28 g) butter to create a mixture that's dry and crumbly. Add this flour mixture to the prepared yeast mixture, and stir together until the mixture begins to form a dough, using your clean, floured hands if necessary to work the dough together.

* Turn dough out onto a lightly floured work surface and knead for about 5 minutes, until smooth and elastic. Form dough into a ball and place inside a greased bowl. Cover and set in a warm place for 1 to 2 hours, until doubled in size.

* Grease an 8 x 8-inch (20 x 20 cm) glass baking dish. Punch down dough with your fist and turn it out onto a floured work surface. Flatten dough into a 9 x 9-inch (23 x 23 cm) square that's ½ inch (13 mm) thick and cut out 3-inch (7.6 cm) rounds. Rework scraps of dough into a new ½-inch (13 mm)-thick piece, and repeat cutting process until you have used up the dough and created 9 rounds. Place them close together in prepared dish, smooshing and pressing them together as necessary, and score the middle of the rounds with a knife. Brush the outsides with remaining tablespoon (14 g) of butter and cover dish with a towel. Let rest for another hour in a warm place.

* Preheat oven to 350°F (180°C, or gas mark 4). Bake for 15 to 20 minutes, until golden on top and around the sides; be careful not to overbake. Remove from oven, let cool in pan for 5 minutes, and then remove rolls to wire racks to cool. Serve with butter and, if desired, honey.

Yield: 9 rolls

¼ cup (60 ml) warm water (100 to 110°F [37 to 43°C])

2 tablespoons (40 g) honey

1 packet (2¼ teaspoons [9 g]) active dry yeast

2¾ to 3 cups (344 to 375 g) all-purpose einkorn flour, plus more for dusting

¾ teaspoon sea salt

½ cup (120 ml) warm milk

3 tablespoons (43 g) butter, melted, divided

WHOLE-GRAIN DINNER ROLLS

Yield: 12 rolls

These hearty dinner rolls take the nutty, grainy flavor of whole-grain einkorn flour and showcase it in yeasty, doughy rolls baked alongside one another in a small pan.

* Proof yeast by whisking it with warm water and honey in a bowl and letting sit 10 minutes or longer, until frothy and bubbly. If yeast hasn't activated in that time, let it rest longer or start over. Don't skip this; if the yeast shows no activity, it is likely dead, and your bread won't rise. Meanwhile, stir together 3¼ cups (325 g) flour, salt, milk, and 2 tablespoons (28 g) butter in a large bowl. Add cooled yeast mixture to the flour mixture and stir together until the mixture begins to come together. If dough is still sticky, add up to another ¼ cup (31 g) of flour and work mixture together.

* Turn dough out onto a lightly floured work surface and knead for 5 minutes. Form dough into a ball; place inside a greased bowl in a warm place for 1 to 2 hours, until puffed and risen. If, after 2 hours, the ball hasn't risen at all, turn it back out onto a floured surface, knead for 5 minutes, and return to oiled bowl for another 1 to 2 hours.

* Grease a 9 x 12-inch (23 x 30 cm) glass baking dish. Punch down dough with your fist and turn it out onto a floured work surface. Flatten dough into a 11-inch (28 cm) square that's ½ inch (13 mm) thick and cut out 3-inch (7.6 cm) rounds. Rework scraps of dough into a new ½-inch (13 mm)-thick piece, and repeat cutting process until you have used up the dough and created 12 rounds. Place them close together in prepared dish, smooshing and pressing them together as necessary, and score the middle of the rounds with a knife. Brush the outsides with remaining tablespoon (14 g) of butter and cover dish with a towel. Let rest for another hour in a warm place.

* Preheat oven to 350°F (180°C, or gas mark 4). Bake rolls for 15 to 20 minutes, until golden; don't overbake. Remove from oven, let cool in pan for 5 minutes, and remove rolls to wire racks to cool. Serve with butter and, if desired, honey.

Ingredients:

1 packet (2¼ teaspoons [9 g]) active dry yeast

¼ cup (60 ml) warm water (100 to 110°F [37 to 43°C])

2 tablespoons (40 g) honey

3¼ to 3½ cups (325 to 350 g) freshly milled, sifted einkorn flour

¾ teaspoon sea salt

½ cup (120 ml) warm milk

3 tablespoons (42 g) butter, melted, divided, plus more for brushing

FOCACCIA WITH CARAMELIZED ONIONS AND TOMATOES

It's hard to think of anything prettier emerging from the oven than a large, dimpled focaccia like this one. Soft and pillowy, studded with tomatoes and caramelized onions, it's as eye-catching as it is heady with the scent of garlic and herbs.

* Proof yeast by whisking it with 1 cup (235 ml) warm water and honey in a bowl and letting sit 10 minutes or longer, until frothy and bubbly. If yeast hasn't activated in that time, let it rest longer or start over. Don't skip this; if the yeast shows no activity, it is likely dead and your bread won't rise.

* Meanwhile, warm coconut oil in a large skillet over medium heat. Add onions and cook over medium-low heat, stirring often. Once onions are beginning to caramelize, about 20 minutes, remove from heat.

* To the yeast mixture, stir in 2 teaspoons salt, remaining water, and 2 cups (250 g) flour. The mixture will look wet and lumpy, like porridge. Stir in more flour until the mixture begins to come together. Use floured hands to knead dough in bowl for 2 to 3 minutes, until soft and elastic but still slightly sticky. Place the ball of dough in an oiled bowl for an hour, or until doubled.

* Preheat oven to 450°F (230°C, or gas mark 8). Drizzle a little olive oil on your fingers and use them to turn dough out onto a parchment-lined baking sheet, forming it into an 11 x 13-inch (23 x 33 cm) rectangle. Use your fingers to press deep dimples all over the dough; drizzle with half the olive oil. Top with coarse salt, Italian herbs, caramelized onions, grated garlic, halved grape tomatoes (cut side down), and Pecorino cheese.

* Bake for 15 to 20 minutes, until golden, and brush edges with remaining olive oil. Let cool slightly before cutting. Serve warm or at room temperature.

Yield: 16 servings

1 packet (2¼ teaspoons [9 g]) active dry yeast

2 cups (475 ml) warm water (about 100 to 105°F), divided

1 teaspoon honey

1 tablespoon (13 g) coconut oil

1 small or half a large onion (4 ounces, or 115 g), sliced

2 teaspoons sea salt

4 to 5 cups (500 to 625 g) all-purpose einkorn flour

2 tablespoons (28 ml) olive oil, divided

1 teaspoon coarse salt

1 tablespoon (2 g) dried Italian herbs (e.g. basil, rosemary, oregano, and/or parsley)

2 cloves garlic, grated

1½ cups (110 g) grape tomatoes, halved

¼ cup (25 g) grated Pecorino cheese

ROSEMARY BREADSTICKS

These long, doughy breadsticks are the ideal accompaniment to both salad and soup, where they're great for sopping up extra juices. What makes them unique is the cream cheese worked into the dough, which turns ordinary breadsticks into what tastes almost like refined pastries. Studded with rosemary and salt, they're as flavorful as they are addictive.

* In a large bowl, combine water, yeast, ginger powder, and 1 teaspoon sugar. Let sit for 10 minutes, until frothy and bubbly. Stir in einkorn flour, remaining sugar, and salt, until mixture becomes a floppy, wrinkly dough. Cut in butter with a pastry cutter or 2 forks; the dough will not look or behave like pie dough, so you're not shooting for the butter to be small pebbles throughout; rather, cut in the butter until all of its pieces are broken up and small, spread throughout. Next, fold in Pecorino and cream cheese, using your floured hands to work the dough together until mixed. Form mixture into a ball, kneading and working it together right in the bowl, about 2 or 3 minutes. Place the soft ball of dough in an oiled bowl, cover with a towel, and let rest for 20 minutes.

* Preheat oven to 425°F (220°C, or gas mark 7) and line 2 baking sheets with parchment paper. Pinch off 2-inch (5 cm) balls of dough, and roll them into 10-inch (25 cm)-long logs that are roughly 1 inch (2.5 cm) thick. Place the logs on parchment paper.

* In a small bowl, whisk together 1 egg white and a teaspoon of water. Brush this mixture on prepared breadsticks. Sprinkle rosemary and salt on top. Bake breadsticks for 10 to 15 minutes, until crisp and golden. Serve warm, brushed with melted butter.

Recipe Note

• Note that the recipe calls for 1 to 2 tablespoons (18 to 36 g) of coarse salt. Using 1 gives a light, salt-kissed flavor, perfect with salads; using 2 makes them extra salty, as a nice foil to creamy soup.

Yield: 13 breadsticks

FOR THE BREADSTICKS:

1 cup (235 ml) warm water (100 to 110°F [37 to 43°C])

1 packet (2¼ teaspoons [9 g]) active dry yeast

¼ teaspoon ginger powder

4 teaspoons (18 g) coconut sugar, Sucanat, or honey, divided

3½ cups (438 g) all-purpose einkorn flour

½ teaspoon sea salt

3 tablespoons (42 g) butter, cold and cubed

2 tablespoons (12 g) grated Pecorino

⅔ cup (100 g) cream cheese, crumbled

FOR THE BREADSTICK TOPPING:

1 egg white

1 teaspoon water

2 tablespoons (3 g) chopped fresh rosemary (or 1 tablespoon [3 g] dried)

1 to 2 tablespoons (18 to 36 g) coarse salt

1 tablespoon (14 g) butter, melted, for brushing

SOFT, PILLOWY PITA POCKETS

Yield: 8 pitas

1 packet (2¼ teaspoons [9 g]) active dry yeast

¾ cup (175 ml) warm water (100 to 110°F [37 to 43°C])

1 tablespoon (20 g) honey

2½ to 3 cups (313 to 375 g) all-purpose einkorn flour, plus more for dusting

½ teaspoon baking powder

1 teaspoon olive oil, plus more for oiling bowl

1½ teaspoons sea salt

*P*itas were one of the first recipes we tried with einkorn, the two of us alone in the kitchen one afternoon, forming balls of dough and watching them puff. What goes into the hot oven as a round of dough emerges, minutes later, as an inflated pillow, perfect for dipping in hummus or stuffing as you like.

* Proof yeast by combining it with warm water and honey in a large bowl, whisking together, and letting sit 10 minutes or longer, until frothy and bubbly. If yeast hasn't activated in that time, let it rest longer or start over. Don't skip this step; if the yeast shows no activity, it is likely dead, and this will keep your pitas from rising.

* Stir in 2½ cups (313 g) flour, baking powder, olive oil, and salt. At first, the mixture may look dry, but it will come together enough for you to use your clean hands to work it together into a ball, pressing and shaping it together. If it doesn't, add a tablespoon (15 ml) of water at a time to make it workable. If it's too wet, add up to another ½ cup (63 g) flour, until workable. Knead dough in bowl for 5 minutes. Place the ball of dough in an oiled bowl, cover with a towel, and let rest until doubled in size, about an hour.

* Divide dough into 8 equal balls. On lightly floured parchment, roll the balls into 5 to 6-inch (13 to 15 cm) circles that are about ⅛ inch (3 mm) thick. Cut out parchment around the pitas.

* Preheat oven to 500°F (260°C, or gas mark 10), and place a baking stone or baking pan inside. Let pitas rest on the counter while oven warms. After 30 minutes, use a pizza peel or large spatula to slide the parchment-lined pitas directly onto the preheated stone or pan, working with a few at a time. Bake pitas for 4 minutes each, until puffed and golden. Enjoy!

Recipe Note

• *In a rush? You can skip the hour rise time—your pitas won't be as soft, but they will be fast flatbreads.*

SIMPLE HOMEMADE TORTILLAS

Yield: 12 to 14 tortillas

Tim's sister gave us a tortilla press that makes flattening tortillas an easy process, but, with or without a press, these tortillas are the definition of simple. The first time we made them, we kept saying we wish we'd done it sooner, loving their soft, golden exterior as much as the thrill of watching them form! These einkorn tortillas are easily stuffed for tacos or enchiladas and make excellent quesadillas for an easy lunch or snack.

* In a medium-size bowl, stir together flour, olive oil, salt, and warm water. Using clean hands, work the mixture together into a ball of dough, kneading it in the bowl until it comes together. Set the ball in the bowl and cover with a towel; let rest for 15 to 30 minutes.

* On a floured surface or large piece of parchment paper, divide the dough into 12 to 14 balls, each about 1½-inches (3.8 cm) wide.

* Heat a cast iron skillet over medium heat on the stove. If using a tortilla press, line both sides of the press with plastic wrap, and flatten 1 dough round between the press. If not using a tortilla press, use a rolling pin and a floured surface to roll 1 dough round into a 5 to 6-inch (13 to 15 cm) circle.

* Working with one at a time, place a flattened tortilla on the hot skillet. Within a minute or two, you should start seeing a lot of bubbles forming on the top of the dough. At this point, use kitchen tongs or a spatula to flip the tortilla and cook for right around a minute on the other side, until both sides are golden, with brown spots, and firm. Remove tortilla to a clean towel and cover to keep warm. Repeat rolling and cooking process with remaining dough.

2¼ cups (280 g) all-purpose einkorn flour, plus up to ¼ cup (31 g) more

¼ cup (60 ml) olive oil or melted coconut oil (or a combination of the two)

½ teaspoon sea salt

½ cup (120 ml) warm water (100 to 110°F [37 to 43°C])

AVOCADO PARATHAS

Yield: 8 parathas

vocado parathas are simple Indian frybreads with a pale green color and a slight kick of spice, perfect alongside a meal with lots of sauce for dipping.

* In a medium bowl, mash together avocado flesh, lemon juice, and salt, until there are no longer any firm pieces and everything is a uniform texture throughout. Mash in the turmeric, cumin, ginger powder, and red pepper flakes. Then, add ½ cup (63 g) of einkorn flour and, using your clean hands, work the mixture together into a dough. Add up to another ½ cup (63 g) of flour if needed. The dough is ready when the bowl is clean, with all the mixture absorbing into the dough, and the dough is smooth and elastic. The dough may be covered for an hour at this point at room temperature, covered and chilled overnight in the fridge, or used right away.

* When ready to cook the parathas, warm a cast iron skillet over medium heat. Divide dough into 8 equal pieces, and roll each one into a ball in your hands, setting it on a floured surface. Using a tortilla press (or a floured surface and a rolling pin), flatten each ball of dough into a thin 5 to 6-inch (13 to 15 cm) round (about ⅟₁₆ inch [1.5 mm] thick). If at any point the dough becomes sticky, add extra flour to your hands as you roll it between your hands, letting it absorb into the dough.

* Sauté the rounds on the heated skillet, one at a time, flipping frequently and adding oil to the pan as you do. Each paratha should take 3 to 6 minutes to cook—you'll see brown spots dotting each side once done. Move cooked parathas to a towel or covered dish to stay warm. Leftover parathas may be stored in a refrigerated airtight container for up to a week.

1 medium (150 g) avocado, pitted and peeled

2 teaspoons fresh lemon juice

½ teaspoon sea salt

½ teaspoon turmeric

½ teaspoon cumin

½ teaspoon ginger powder

⅛ to ¼ teaspoon of crushed red pepper flakes

½ to 1 cup (63 to 125 g) all-purpose einkorn flour, plus more for flouring surfaces

2 tablespoons (26 g) coconut oil, melted, for oiling pan

SOURDOUGH SLIDER BUNS

As written, this recipe yields small, 3-inch (7.6 cm) buns that crack on top while baking and feature a sweet, buttery flavor so enticing, you may want to eat these on their own. If you want larger buns for full-size burgers, simply form the balls into the size you like. Also, if you prefer smooth tops for your buns (with no cracks on top), skip the honey butter and herbs, and brush a little butter on the buns after baking instead.

* Combine sourdough starter, sugar, oil, egg, and salt in a large bowl. Add flour, 1 cup (125 g) at a time, until the dough becomes too stiff to stir. Use your hands to knead it into a workable dough, adding more flour as needed, kneading for about 5 to 10 minutes. Dough should be soft and elastic, not sticky. Knead in the bowl a few times and then move to an oiled bowl to rest, turning it to cover in the oil. Cover and let dough rise until doubled in size, about 2 hours.

* Pinch off pieces of dough into 3-inch (7.6 cm) balls; you'll get about 10. Stretch the dough across the top and bottoms of the balls to make them as smooth and taut as possible; this will help the buns form properly as they bake. Place on parchment-lined baking sheets and flatten slightly. Let rise for another hour; they might not become much bigger, but letting them rest will aid their rise in the oven.

* Preheat oven to 375°F (190°C, or gas mark 5). In a small bowl, mix together butter and honey and brush rolls with this mixture. If using, add dried herbs to the tops of each roll for extra flavor.

* Bake rolls until lightly golden, 15 to 20 minutes, rotating pan halfway through. Slice one in half horizontally to double-check doneness; let buns cool before slicing and filling as you like.

Yield: Ten 3-inch (7.6 cm) buns

1½ cups (397 g) fed sourdough starter

⅓ cup (53 g) coconut sugar

2 tablespoons (28 ml) olive oil

1 egg, lightly beaten

1 teaspoon sea salt

2½ to 3 cups (313 to 375 g) all-purpose einkorn flour

1 tablespoon (14 g) butter, melted, for brushing

1 tablespoon (15 g) honey, for brushing

1 to 2 tablespoons (4 to 8 g) dried herbs, such as Simply Organic Garlic 'n' Herb, optional

PRETZEL ROLLS

These dinner rolls feature a firm, browned exterior dimpled with salt and a soft, yeasty interior that marries well with butter. Form them a little larger, and you have pretzel buns for burgers or sandwiches. Roll them into logs and form them into pretzels, and you have traditional Bavarian-style pretzels to dip in sauce.

* Proof yeast by combining it with warm water and honey in a large bowl, whisking together, and letting sit 10 minutes or longer, until frothy and bubbly. If yeast hasn't activated in that time, let it rest longer or start over. Don't skip this step; if the yeast shows no activity, it is likely dead, and this will keep your rolls from rising.

* Stir melted butter into yeast mixture and let rest 5 to 10 minutes. Stir in salt and flour, use your hands to form the mixture into a shaggy dough, and turn dough onto a floured surface, kneading 5 minutes, adding more flour if needed. Form dough into a ball and place in an oiled bowl. Cover with a clean towel and place in a warm place until doubled in size (about an hour).

* When dough is ready, preheat oven to 425°F (220°C, or gas mark 7) and line 2 baking sheets with parchment paper. Divide the dough into 12 to 16 equal pieces, and form each piece into a ball about 2 to 3 inches (5 to 7.6 cm) wide, stretching the top simultaneously to each side and tucking the ends under. Place the balls, seam side down, on the parchment-lined baking sheets.

* Bring 3 quarts (2.8 L) water to a boil and slowly add baking soda. Boil the rolls one at a time, rolling to cover, about 30 seconds. Remove back to the baking sheets with a slotted spoon. Brush rolls with beaten egg and sprinkle with sea salt. Cut an X into the top of each roll.

* Bake 12 to 15 minutes, rotating sheets halfway through, until rolls are firm and beautifully brown.

Yield: 12 to 16 rolls

1 packet (2¼ teaspoons [9 g]) active dry yeast

1 cup (235 ml) warm water (105 to 115°F [40 to 46°C])

1 tablespoon (20 g) honey

4 tablespoons (55 g) unsalted butter, melted

2½ teaspoons salt

3½ cups (438 g) all-purpose einkorn flour

Olive oil, for bowl

3 quarts (2.8 L) water

¾ cup (170 g) baking soda

1 egg, beaten

Coarse salt, for sprinkling

CLASSIC ARTISAN SOURDOUGH BREAD

Usually, we know better than to make any grand sweeping claims with bread—but, truly, we think this is some of the best bread we have ever had. Most artisan sourdoughs utilizing ancient grains combine other flours, gluten, or enhancers in order to achieve the artisan loaf. We wanted to create a beautiful sourdough that was 100 percent einkorn to protect some of the benefits it offers over other varieties of wheat or gluten. We feel that some of the best parts of einkorn are only enhanced by the long-ferment process outlined below.

* **Day 1:** For the preferment, in a large bowl, combine sourdough starter, flour, water, and ginger powder. Mix until just combined. The mixture should be a very thick, sticky batter. Cover the bowl with plastic wrap and place a towel on top to keep light out (to prevent oxidation). Let mixture sit on the counter overnight, or 8 to 12 hours.

* **Day 2:** After its overnight rest, the preferment should be at least twice its size and bubbly. Add 1 cup (125 g) of flour, water, sea salt, and honey. Stir until all ingredients are incorporated. The resulting mixture will still be very sticky. Pour the remaining 1 cup (125 g) of flour out onto a counter or workspace, flour hands well, and pour out the dough onto the floured counter. Begin to knead the dough gently by working the flour into the dough, adding more as needed to keep it from sticking to the counter. Knead for about 5 minutes until most of the flour is worked into the dough. The dough should be smooth and semi-elastic but still a bit tacky or sticky.

* Spread or stretch out the dough into a rectangle, about 16 x 8 inches (40 x 20 cm). Fold one of the short sides in like a letter, then fold the top halfway down. Fold the other short side all the way over, and lastly stretch and fold the bottom flap over the top. Flip over and, using your hands to cup the sides, form a tight ball with the dough. Place the ball into a well-floured towel-lined 8-inch (20 cm) rising bowl or brotform; you can use rice flour to flour the towel as it is excellent to keep dough from sticking, but einkorn flour works as well. Cover with the ends of the towel gently and if possible place the whole bowl or brotform into a plastic bag to keep the moisture in. Place in the refrigerator for 24 hours.

Yield: 1 loaf

HELPFUL TOOLS

Kitchen scale

8-inch (20 cm) rising bowl or basket (brotform)

Active sourdough starter

Baking stone

Baker's peel

DAY 1—PREFERMENT

½ cup (110 g) active sourdough starter maintained at 120 percent hydration (see note)

3 cups (375 g) all-purpose einkorn flour

1 cup (240 ml) purified water

¼ teaspoon organic ginger powder

DAY 2—COLD FERMENT

2 cups (250 g) all-purpose einkorn flour, divided

½ cup (115 g or ml) purified water

2 teaspoons sea salt

2 tablespoons (40 g) honey

Extra einkorn flour or rice flour for dusting surface

DAY 3

Water

Recipe Note

• *To maintain your starter at 120 percent hydration, simply add ½ cup (120 ml) of water for every ¾ (100 grams) of flour (or any division of that such as ¼ cup [60 grams] water to ⅓ cup [50 grams] flour). After a few feedings at this ratio your starter should be an easy to maintain batter.*

✳ **Day 3:** Place a baking stone in the oven on the middle rack and preheat to 500°F (260°C, or gas mark 10). Allow oven/stone to heat for at least 45 minutes before baking bread.

✳ About 15 minutes before baking bread, either place a large baking dish with 2 inches (5 cm) of water on the lowest rack, or place multiple oven-safe bowls with 2 inches (5 cm) of water on the lowest rack (my preferred method). The idea is to create steam in the oven, which is most important in the first 20 minutes of baking to help the rise and to form a beautiful crust. Alternatively, you may preheat a Dutch oven (with lid) and bake the bread in the Dutch oven, which will also keep the moisture in, removing the lid after the first 25 minutes.

✳ After placing your water pan on the lower rack (about 15 minutes before you bake the bread), remove the bread from the refrigerator and take the bowl out of the bag. Using a baker's peel or cutting board lined with parchment paper, place it on top of the bowl and invert the bowl onto the lined peel/cutting board. Remove the bowl and the towel gently. Slash the top of the dough with a sharp knife or a serrated knife, about ½ inch (13 mm) deep, ensuring that the dough separates slightly at the slash. You may slash in whatever pattern you like, but I recommend at least 3 slashes. Let sit at room temperature for 10 to 15 minutes.

✳ Carefully slide the dough onto the hot stone in the oven (or into the hot Dutch oven). Reduce the temperature to 475°F (250°C or gas mark 9) and bake for 25 minutes (keep oven closed for the whole 25 minutes to keep as much steam in the oven as possible). After 25 minutes, reduce temperature to 450°F (230°C) and bake for 15 to 20 minutes. If the bread seems to be cooking unevenly on one side, carefully rotate the bread to cook evenly for the remaining 15 to 20 minutes. The crust should be very dark, with the slashes or breaks showing a golden glow. The bottom of the loaf should sound hollow when tapped.

✳ Remove the bread from the oven and cool on a rack for at least 1 hour before slicing. The crust should be crunchy with a tender and moist inner crumb (not too tight, but with some small pockets and holes).

CHERRY WALNUT SOURDOUGH BOULE

This recipe uses the same method as the artisan sourdough, but for a much sweeter result. Note that, as in our other sourdough recipes, weighing in grams is preferred.

* **Day 1:** Follow recipe as directed in the Classic Artisan Sourdough (page 66).

* **Day 2:** Follow the Classic Artisan Sourdough recipe up through stretching into a rectangle. Spread half of the dried cherries and walnuts on the rectangle. Fold the short end in like a letter and spread more cherries and walnuts on the fold. Fold the top halfway down and spread more cherries and walnuts on the fold. Fold the other short end all the way over and add the remaining cherries and walnuts. Lastly, stretch and fold the bottom over the top. If you have extra cherries or walnuts or did not have enough don't worry; it does not have to be exact. Flip the dough over and using your hands to cup the sides, form a circle or ball with the dough. Continue on with placing the dough in the refrigerator overnight as directed in the Artisan Sourdough recipe.

* **Day 3:** Follow Artisan Sourdough recipe.

Yield: 1 loaf

DAY 1–PREFERMENT

1 cup (220 g) active sourdough starter at 120 percent hydration

3 cups (375 g) all-purpose einkorn flour

1 cup (230 g) purified water

¼ teaspoon organic ginger powder

DAY 2–COLD FERMENT

2 cups (250 g) all-purpose einkorn flour

¼ cup (57 g) purified water

⅓ cup (53 g) Sucanat or unrefined sugar

2 teaspoons sea salt

1 cup (160 g) whole dried cherries

¾ cup chopped walnuts (85 g)

WHOLE-GRAIN SOURDOUGH

This recipe variation essentially uses the same method as the artisan sourdough, but it takes into account some of the differences when using fresh ground flour from whole-grain einkorn berries.

* Follow full Classic Artisan Sourdough recipe directions on page 66, using proportions listed here.

Yield: 1 loaf

DAY 1–PREFERMENT

½ cup (110 g) active sourdough starter at 120 percent hydration

3 cups (300 g) freshly ground einkorn flour

1 cup (230 g) purified water

Dash of ginger

DAY 2–COLD FERMENT

½ cup (115 g) purified water

2 cups (200 g) flour + 1 cup (100 g)
    for turning out and kneading in

2 teaspoons sea salt

2 tablespoons (40 g) honey

GARLIC CHEESE SOURDOUGH CROUTONS

*N*ext time you want to give your salad a lift—although, actually, these are addictive enough to eat on their own—make these croutons. Not only do they make your kitchen smell like an Italian restaurant while they bake, but they also marry tangy bread with cheese and garlic, a winning combination if we've ever known one.

✳ Preheat oven to 300°F (150°C, or gas mark 2). Melt butter with olive oil and grated garlic in a saucepan over medium-low heat. Place the cubed sourdough bread in a large bowl and pour warmed butter mixture on top. Add Pecorino cheese, parsley, and salt; stir together or massage with clean fingers to combine. Spread on a baking sheet in a single layer and bake for 45 minutes to an hour, tossing at least once. Croutons are done when they are crisp and golden, with a strong crunch when you bite in.

Yield: 2 cups (200 g) of croutons

3 tablespoons (42 g) unsalted butter

2 tablespoons (30 ml) olive oil

4 cloves of garlic, grated

3 cups (200 to 220 g) cubed einkorn sourdough bread (cubed into ½-inch to 1-inch [13 mm to 2.5 cm] squares)

¼ cup (25 g) grated Pecorino cheese

⅓ cup (14 g) chopped parsley

½ teaspoon sea salt

HERBED BREAD CRUMBS

*T*he fringe benefit of testing dozens of bread recipes is, by necessity, learning dozens of ways to use that bread up. Here, for example is a simple, flavorful way to make homemade bread crumbs, which comes in handy for many recipes in this book, such as our Italian meatballs.

✳ Blend the toast pieces in a food processor until very fine. Add herbs and salt and pepper and pulse to combine. Store bread crumbs in the fridge in a closed mason jar or sealed plastic bag.

Yield: Approximately 1½ cups (146 g) bread crumbs

5 slices Soft Sandwich Loaf (page 45), toasted and broken into pieces

¼ cup (13 g) chopped fresh herbs such as rosemary, thyme, or basil

½ teaspoon sea salt

½ teaspoon black pepper

CHAPTER 4

Here is the beauty of small bites: Because of their small proportions, they allow you to taste more items as you like them. When you go to a cocktail party or are served hors d'oeuvres at a wedding, you may sample a dozen different foods, and, in so doing, experience new tastes you enjoy. You may go back twice for the mini quiche. You may eat your fill of bruschetta. With einkorn, appetizers take the form of crostini and flatbreads, quesadillas and hand pies, among other bites. But while they're all designed to be finger foods, that doesn't mean they can't be main dishes. In other words, if you find yourself alone in the kitchen on Sunday nights, snacking for dinner, we won't tell anybody.

❖ Curried Cauliflower Puff Pies with Parsley Mint Chutney 72
❖ Caramelized Onion, Mushroom, and Mozzarella Quesadillas..... 74
❖ Peach, Basil, and Ricotta Flatbreads 75

❖ Sweet Potato and Onion Crostini........................... 77
❖ Tomato Avocado Crostini 77
❖ Lettuce Wraps with Peanut Sauce 78
❖ Herbed Sourdough Crackers 81

❖ Olive Tapenade......................... 82
❖ Tomato Pastry Tart.................... 84

CURRIED CAULIFLOWER PUFF PIES
WITH PARSLEY MINT CHUTNEY

This might be the most elaborate recipe in the book, but, taste-wise, we promise it's worth all the effort. After all the steps and chilling times are completed and the pies are baked, they emerge from the oven, crisp and golden, with buttery crusts and spicy filling that pair perfectly with the cooling, refreshing chutney filled with parsley and mint.

* Start by making the pastry dough: In a large bowl, combine flour, salt, and sugar. Cut in cubed butter with a pastry cutter, until the butter is broken up into big chunks throughout, about 15 to 20 seconds. Add 4 tablespoons (60 ml) of water and stir mixture together until it's well mixed; if the mixture still looks dry and if attempting to gather it together with your hands won't work, stir in another tablespoon (15 ml) of water; repeat once more if needed. Using clean, floured fingers, form mixture into ball of dough.

Yield: Thirteen 2.5-inch (6 cm) hand pies

FOR THE DOUGH PASTRY:

1¾ cups (175 g) freshly ground, sifted einkorn flour

½ teaspoon sea salt

1 teaspoon sugar (coconut sugar, Sucanat, or other sugar)

2 sticks (225 g) butter, cold and cubed into ½ tablespoons (7 g)

4 to 6 tablespoons (60 to 90 ml) water (see note)

Recipe Notes

• *Note that different kitchen temperatures and humidity levels may affect how much water to add to the dough, so adjust the water as needed.*

• *To use all-purpose einkorn with this recipe, simply swap in the same weight of all-purpose flour for the freshly milled, whole-grain flour.*

* Turn this dough out onto a floured surface and use a floured rolling pin to roll into an 8½ x 11-inch (22 x 28 cm) rectangle, like the size of a piece of paper. With the short side facing you, fold the bottom third up, then the top third over that, like you were folding a letter. Turn the dough clockwise 90 degrees and repeat. Wrap dough in plastic and chill 30 minutes.

* Remove chilled dough, and on a floured surface using a floured rolling pin, roll it out into an 8½ x 11-inch (22 x 28 cm) rectangle again. With the short side facing you, fold the bottom third up, then the top third over that, like you were folding a letter. Turn the dough clockwise 90 degrees and repeat. Wrap dough in plastic and chill 1 hour.

* Meanwhile, to make the cauliflower filling: Warm coconut oil in a large stockpot over medium heat, until hot. Add onion and spices, stir, and let this mixture cook for about 5 minutes, so the onions slightly soften and the spices toast. Add cauliflower, and toss to coat. Add stock, and cook mixture on medium heat for 15 to 20 minutes, until the stock gets absorbed. Add spinach, tossing it with the stock until warm. Remove from heat.

* When ready to make the hand pies, preheat oven to 375°F (190°C, or gas mark 5) and line two baking sheets with parchment paper. Pull dough from fridge and use a pastry cutter or sharp knife to separate dough into 2 equal pieces. Wrap 1 in the plastic and place it back in the fridge. Take the other and roll it out, on a floured surface, to be 8½ x 11 inches (22 x 28 cm) in size and about $\frac{1}{16}$ inch (1.5 mm) thick. Cut out rounds with a 2.5-inch (6 cm) biscuit cutter or other cookie cutter or floured glass, and place them on parchment. Repeat with second half of dough.

* Spoon cauliflower filling into half of the rounds, leaving a ¼-inch to ½-inch (6 to 13 mm) border around the edges. Brush those edges with water and place an empty round on top of each filled one, pressing down around the sides and sticking the top and bottom dough together. Use a fork to press the edges together. Brush pastries with egg wash and slit the tops with a knife.

* Bake for 15 to 25 minutes, until golden brown on top. While pastries bake, make the parsley mint chutney: combine all ingredients into a food processor and process until onion and herbs are very finely diced and incorporated. The resulting mixture should not be smooth or chunky, but have the texture of the finely diced onions.

* Serve pastries warm, with mint parsley chutney on top or on the side.

FOR THE CAULIFLOWER FILLING:

1 tablespoon (13 g) coconut oil

1 cup (160 g) chopped onion (from about 1 small or ½ large onion)

½ teaspoon ground cumin

½ teaspoon ground coriander

½ teaspoon cardamom

½ teaspoon turmeric

½ teaspoon sea salt

½ teaspoon black pepper

¼ teaspoon garlic powder

¼ teaspoon red chili powder

½ head of cauliflower, chopped (or 4 cups [400 g] chopped)

⅓ cup (83 ml) stock

6 ounces (170 g) frozen spinach

FOR THE EGG WASH:

1 egg yolk

1 teaspoon water

FOR THE MINT CHUTNEY:

1½ cups (150 g) quartered onion

2 cups (34 g) parsley

⅔ cup (8 g) mint leaves

¾ teaspoon red chili pepper flakes

½ teaspoon sea salt

Dash or crack of black pepper

1 to 2 tablespoons (15 to 30 ml) lemon juice, to taste

CARAMELIZED ONION, MUSHROOM, AND MOZZARELLA QUESADILLAS

Quesadillas are one of our go-to quick meals—all you need are tortillas, some cheese, and a little imagination. This version, which features cremini mushrooms, caramelized onions, spinach, mozzarella, and basil, is a little like pizza and a little like a casserole. Every bite is filled with cheesy, vegetable-laden goodness.

* In a large skillet, warm a tablespoon (13 g) of coconut oil over medium heat. Add mushrooms, onions, salt, and crushed red chili flakes. Cook for around 10 minutes, or until wilted and translucent, stirring once or twice. Add spinach leaves and stir together over the heat until the spinach is nicely coated with oil and wilts. Turn off heat and remove pan to another burner to cool slightly.

* Warm a cast iron pan or other skillet on the stove over medium heat. Place 1 tortilla on the pan, followed by a third of the mushroom-onion mixture, then slices of mozzarella, then 3 leaves of basil. Top with another einkorn tortilla. Let cook until cheese is beginning to melt. Use a metal spatula to flip the quesadilla to the other side and continue cooking until cheese is gooey and melted and the quesadilla holds together well. Remove to a plate and cut into quarters. Repeat process with remaining ingredients.

* Serve quesadilla quarters on a large plate, garnished with torn pieces of the remaining basil leaves.

Yield: 3 quesadillas

1 tablespoon (13 g) coconut oil

1 cup (70 g) sliced cremini mushrooms

½ cup (80 g) sliced onions

½ teaspoon sea salt

½ teaspoon crushed red chili flakes

½ cup (15 g) baby spinach leaves

6 Simple Homemade Tortillas (page 60), 6 inches (15 cm) each

1 cup (125 g) sliced, good-quality mozzarella

½ cup (8 g) torn fresh basil leaves

PEACH, BASIL, AND RICOTTA FLATBREADS

Those of you who are looking for quick recipe ideas, here you go. It's true the flatbreads involve a dough, but, we promise, there never was a faster one. If you want a true cracker flatbread crust, you could reduce the amount of flour slightly and let the dough bake a few extra minutes; if you want a softer, pita-like crust, follow the recipe as written here.

* Preheat the oven to 450°F (230°C, or gas mark 8). If you have a baking stone, stick it in the oven as it preheats, on the middle rack (or use a standard baking sheet).

* In a medium or large bowl, combine einkorn flour, basil, baking powder, and salt. Make a well in the center and add the water and olive oil. Stir the flour into the center with a wooden spoon until a dough forms. Once it comes together, knead the dough a few times right in the bowl, creating a nice round of dough.

* Split the dough up into 3 equal pieces. On floured parchment paper or another service, roll each piece of dough into an 8-inch (20 cm) circle. Brush with oil and sprinkle with salt.

* Bake each round of dough, 8 to 13 minutes, until it is the consistency you like (less time yields a softer, pita-like crust; longer time yields a crisp, crackery crust). Once each flatbread bakes, transfer it to a counter or rack to cool.

* Top each flatbread with enough ricotta to cover it, then basil leaves, then peaches. Sprinkle salt and pepper all over the top, and drizzle honey as you like. The flatbreads can be sliced easily with a pizza cutter when they're pita consistency; if yours are more crackery, beware of many crumbs. Serve immediately.

Yield: 3 small flatbreads

FOR THE FLATBREADS:

2 cups (250 g) all-purpose einkorn flour

1½ tablespoons (3 g) torn fresh basil

1 teaspoon baking powder

¾ teaspoon salt, plus more for topping before baking

½ cup (120 ml) water

¼ cup (60 ml) olive oil, plus more for brushing

FOR THE FLATBREAD TOPPINGS:

10 ounces (284 g) whole-milk ricotta

3 to 4 tablespoons (6 to 8 g) torn fresh basil

2 peaches, sliced into thin half circles

Sea salt and black pepper, for dashing all over the top

A few drizzles of honey

◄ TOMATO AVOCADO CROSTINI

*T*his recipe is straight out of Tim's bachelor days, during which he wooed me with the beauty of fresh foods on toast. This crostini involves garlic-rubbed toast, avocado, and tomatoes. Balsamic vinegar, coarse salt, and basil make everything sing.

* Preheat oven to 400°F (200°C or gas mark 6). Lay bread on parchment-lined baking sheet. Brush tops and bottoms with olive oil or ghee. Bake 5 minutes, flip bread slices, and bake 5 to 10 minutes more, until crisp and golden.

* When crostini are still warm, rub cloves of garlic on tops. Lay avocado slices and tomato slices alternately across each one. Drizzle balsamic vinegar and sprinkle salt on top. As the final step before serving, add torn basil.

Yield: 6 servings

6 half-inch-thick (1.25 cm) slices of One-Bowl Butter Bread (page 46)

4 to 6 tablespoons (60 to 90 ml) olive oil or melted ghee

2 cloves of garlic

1 (235 g) ripe avocado, pitted and sliced

2 Roma tomatoes, sliced

2 tablespoons (30 ml) balsamic vinegar

1 tablespoon (18 g) coarse salt

¼ cup (4 g) torn fresh basil leaves

SWEET POTATO AND ONION CROSTINI

*T*hese crostini place some of fall's best flavors atop golden, toasted bread. Combined with the creamy ricotta and chopped rosemary, they are hearty, savory treats with a bold crunch.

* Preheat oven to 400°F (200°C or gas mark 6). Lay bread slices on parchment-lined baking sheet and brush tops and bottoms with 6 tablespoons (90 ml) olive oil or ghee. Bake for 5 minutes, flip bread slices, and bake for 5 to 10 minutes more, until crisp and golden.

* Meanwhile, warm remaining 2 tablespoons (30 ml) of olive oil or ghee in a large skillet over medium heat. Add sliced onion, cubed sweet potatoes, and salt, and cook until potatoes are soft and onions are just beginning to brown, about 10 minutes.

* Spread a teaspoon of ricotta on each crostini, top with sweet potato mixture, and sprinkle chopped rosemary and remaining salt on top to serve.

Yield: 6 servings

6 half-inch-thick (1.25 cm) slices of One-Bowl Butter Bread (page 46)

½ cup (120 ml) olive oil or melted ghee, divided

1 cup (200 g) thinly sliced onion (from 1 medium onion)

1 large sweet potato (200 g), peeled and cubed into bite-size pieces

2 teaspoons salt, divided

2 tablespoons (33 g) ricotta

2 teaspoons chopped rosemary

LETTUCE WRAPS WITH PEANUT SAUCE

We love the fresh crunch of vegetable-packed lettuce wraps, especially when they're paired with a sweet and spicy peanut sauce like this one. They're bright and refreshing, they're super flavorful, and they can be fully adapted to your own preferences and tastes. While we've provided measurements for add-ins such as carrots and scallions below, they are meant to be more of a guide than a formula. Feel free to adjust fillings to your tastes.

* In a small saucepan over medium heat, whisk together broth, ginger, garlic, soy sauce, peanut butter, and honey. Once everything is melted and combined, take ¼ cup (75 g) of the mixture and combine it in a bowl with the cooked einkorn berries. Reserve the remaining sauce as a dipping sauce for the lettuce wraps.

* To assemble the wraps, fill each piece of butter lettuce with ⅙ of the berries, then top each one with scallions, carrots, cucumbers, and mung bean sprouts. Set on a platter, either open or rolled, with the extra peanut sauce.

Yield: 6 lettuce wraps

**FOR THE PEANUT SAUCE
(WILL MAKE 1 CUP [300 g]):**

½ cup (120 ml) vegetable broth

1 teaspoon freshly grated ginger

2 teaspoons freshly grated garlic

2 tablespoons (30 ml) organic
soy sauce

3 tablespoons (48 g) creamy, salted
organic peanut butter

1 tablespoon (20 g) raw honey

FOR THE LETTUCE WRAPS:

6 leaves butter lettuce (or other
sturdy lettuce)

1 cup (190 g) Cooked Einkorn Berries
(page 15)

½ cup (46 g) chopped scallions

1 cup (100 g) thin carrot matchsticks
(from 1 large carrot)

1⅓ cups (145 g) cucumber matchsticks
(from ½ cucumber)

1 cup (75 g) mung bean sprouts

HERBED SOURDOUGH CRACKERS

Homemade crackers seem fancy and elaborate, but they are crazy simple to pull together, especially this sourdough version. After you mix together a dough and let it rest for a few hours, you simply roll out dough, cut, butter, and season it, and bake it until dry. We love making these little flatbread crackers with an artisan feel and serving them alongside cheese and fruit.

* In a large bowl, use a wooden spoon to stir together starter, einkorn flour, salt, and olive oil. Cover bowl with plastic wrap and let mixture sit at room temperature for 2 to 4 hours.

* Preheat oven to 350°F (180°C or gas mark 4). Divide dough in half. On 2 floured pieces of parchment, roll each half out to be ¹⁄₁₆ inch (1.5 mm) thick. Slide parchment sheets onto baking sheets. Brush with melted butter or olive oil or ghee. Sprinkle with garlic herb seasonings and salt. Use a pizza cutter to divide the dough into squares and rectangles.

* Bake dough for 15 minutes; then lower temperature to 175°F (80°C or gas mark ½) and bake for 1 to 2 hours. Taste a cracker to see if it's as dry as you'd like; if not, continue baking and check every 30 minutes or so.

Yield: 25 to 30 crackers

FOR THE CRACKERS:

1¼ cup (294 g) 120 percent hydration sourdough discard

1¼ cups (156 g) einkorn flour, plus more for dusting surfaces

½ teaspoon sea salt

¼ cup (60 ml) olive oil, butter, ghee, or coconut oil, melted (if necessary) and cooled

FOR BRUSHING:

2 tablespoons (28 g) melted butter or ghee

2 to 3 tablespoons (9 to 13 g) garlic herb seasonings (such as Simply Organic Garlic 'n Herb)

1 tablespoon (18 g) sea salt

OLIVE TAPENADE

Inspired by Alton Brown's Wheat Berry Tapenade, this einkorn twist makes a wonderful savory appetizer, particularly atop crusty bread.

* Place the olives, capers, mustard, and basil in a food processor and process until finely diced, about 5 to 10 seconds. The resulting mixture should not be smooth—it should still have some texture to it as the olives will be finely diced but not pureed.

* In a separate bowl stir cooked einkorn berries in with the olive mixture until evenly incorporated. Serve atop crusty bread such as the classic einkorn sourdough (page 66).

Yield: 1½ cups (336 g)

1 cup (145 g) kalamata olives

¼ cup (45 g) capers

1 teaspoon Dijon mustard

¼ cup (4 g) torn basil leaves, thyme, or parsley

1 cup (190 g) Cooked Einkorn Berries (page 15)

Recipe Note

• *Don't have kalamatas? Try substituting another blonde or black olive instead.*

TOMATO PASTRY TART

We originally called this a pizza pastry on our blog because it's a little like the love child of a pie and a pizza, if that love child got to change a little and become more refined. With a flaky pastry base and a tangy yogurt topping, it's also a beautiful little appetizer, perfect for slicing into small servings for a party or as a dinner party small bite.

* Preheat oven to 350°F (180°C, or gas mark 4). In a medium bowl, combine flour and salt. Cut in butter with a pastry cutter or forks, until butter is in chunks throughout. Add water and stir mixture until it begins to come together. Use your clean hands to push and press it into a solid ball. If the mixture is too sticky, add a little more flour; if it's too dry, add a little more water.

* On a floured piece of parchment and using a floured rolling pin, roll out dough into a large, rustic shape that's about 8 or 9 inches (20 or 23 cm) in diameter. Fold and press the edges as you would a freeform tart. Slide parchment onto a baking sheet, and bake for 25 minutes, until just cooked and firm. Remove parchment to counter and let cool slightly until you're ready to fill and bake the tart.

* When ready to bake the tart, spoon yogurt onto center, spreading it around the dough in a nice, smooth layer. Next, place the tomato slices all over the yogurt, and add basil throughout. Generously sprinkle salt and pepper over the top. Slide into the oven and bake for 30 to 45 minutes, until the tomatoes are soft and the crust is golden. Drizzle a little of your favorite balsamic vinegar on at the end, slice, and serve.

Yield: 1 tart, or 4 to 6 servings

FOR THE PASTRY TART:

1 cup (125 g) all-purpose einkorn flour, plus more for sprinkling counters

½ teaspoon salt

½ cup (112 g) unsalted butter, cold and cubed

¼ cup (60 ml) water

FOR THE TOPPINGS:

2 to 3 tablespoons (30 to 45 g) whole-milk plain yogurt

½ to 1 large heirloom tomato, stem end sliced off, thinly sliced into large rounds

A handful of fresh basil

Generous sprinkles of salt and pepper

Balsamic vinegar, for drizzling at the end

CHAPTER 5

Einkorn Berry Salads

Truthfully, for a long while, we didn't see the point of grain salads. When you already like leafy greens, what added good can cooked grains impart? But in more recent years, we've begun to appreciate the filling, satisfying power that comes from pairing greens and grains—through salads that leave us full not only quicker, but also longer.

In this salad section, we demonstrate a variety of ways to use einkorn as a lighter course, from cubed bread in panzanellas to cooked berries with kale. In every case, einkorn pairs beautifully with fresh foods and ingredients, lending its distinct flavor as well as rich nutrients to every dish.

❖ Tabbouleh 87
❖ Acorn Squash and Caramelized Onion Salad.............................. 89
❖ Mushroom Salad with Crushed Red Pepper 90
❖ Herbed Tomato Salad 91
❖ Italian-Style Kale and Einkorn Berry Salad 92
❖ Parsley Pesto Caprese Salad 94
❖ Classic Panzanella 95
❖ Radish Panzanella 97
❖ Corn and White Bean Salad 98
❖ Mediterranean Salad 99
❖ Dried Fruit and Toasted Almond Einkorn Berry Salad 100
❖ Butternut Squash Pilaf 102

TABBOULEH

Just as traditional tabbouleh celebrates the bright, fresh flavor that comes from mint, this einkorn version is all about the refreshing, bold flavor of that herb, paired with chewy einkorn berries and fresh ingredients.

* In a medium-size bowl, place the einkorn berries with enough water to cover them and add apple cider vinegar. Soak for at least 4 hours and up to overnight.

* After soaking, strain and rinse the berries. Place the einkorn berries in a saucepan with a cup (235 ml) of water, and bring to a boil over medium heat. Reduce to a simmer, cover, and cook for 30 to 35 minutes, until berries are no longer hard, but slightly chewy. Drain any excess water.

* Combine all ingredients in a large serving bowl. Toss until everything is evenly incorporated and well coated with oil and lemon juice. Adjust seasoning to taste and let sit for at least 30 minutes (the longer it sits, the more the flavors marinate together).

Yield: 4 to 6 servings

½ cup (100 g) einkorn berries

½ teaspoon apple cider vinegar

1 cup (235 ml) water

1 cup (125 g) chopped cucumbers, from about half a cucumber

¾ cup (85 g) chopped tomato

⅔ cup (16 g) chopped parsley

¼ cup (5 g) roughly chopped mint leaves

½ clove garlic, minced or grated

2 tablespoons (30 ml) lemon juice

2 tablespoons (30 ml) olive oil

½ teaspoon sea salt

¼ teaspoon fresh ground black pepper

Recipe Note

• *Because tabbouleh is a forgiving side dish, you can feel free to adjust the herbs as you like here.*

ACORN SQUASH AND CARAMELIZED ONION SALAD

The star of this dish, which would be as perfect at Thanksgiving dinner as on a random weeknight, is the caramelized onion. We've paired it with autumn ingredients such as acorn squash and apples, though it would also work with another type of squash or even sweet potato. Bright and flavorful, this salad is an excellent example of ways einkorn side dishes can steal the show.

* In a medium-size bowl, place the einkorn berries with enough water to cover them and add apple cider vinegar. Soak for at least 4 hours and up to overnight.

* After soaking, strain and rinse the berries and set in a saucepan over medium heat with 1 cup (235 ml) of water. Bring to a boil then reduce to a simmer, cooking until al dente, about 30 to 45 minutes. While the einkorn is cooking, preheat the oven to 350°F (180°C, or gas mark 4). Once the einkorn is done, remove from heat, and strain any excess water.

* In a medium-size bowl, toss the squash with 2 tablespoons (30 ml) of coconut oil and a half a teaspoon each of salt and pepper. Transfer to a baking sheet and roast for 30 minutes, until soft and caramelized.

* Warm remaining 2 tablespoons (30 ml) of coconut oil in a large skillet. Add onions and cook over medium heat, stirring often, adding the remaining ½ teaspoon salt while they cook. This should take around 20 to 30 minutes. Once onions are soft, golden, and caramelized, remove from heat.

* To assemble the salad, toss together cooked einkorn berries, roasted squash, caramelized onion, diced apples, chopped parsley, and grated Pecorino together in a large bowl. Serve warm.

Yield: 4 to 6 servings

1 cup (200 g) einkorn berries

1 teaspoon apple cider vinegar

1 cup water (235 ml)

1½ cups (180 g) peeled and cubed acorn squash (about 1 small squash)

4 tablespoons (60 ml) melted coconut oil or butter, divided

1 teaspoon sea salt, divided, plus more to taste

½ teaspoon black pepper

2¼ cups (225 g) sliced yellow onion

¾ cup (80 g) diced apple (unpeeled)

¼ cup (5 g) chopped parsley

½ cup (50 g) grated Pecorino cheese

MUSHROOM SALAD WITH CRUSHED RED PEPPER

I wasted almost three full decades of my life hating mushrooms, and now I can't get enough of them—thank you, Tim! Along with kale, fermented foods, and, ever so slowly, olives, my husband has opened my eyes to hundreds of ingredients I'd been afraid to keep trying. In this salad, the mushrooms are sautéed until golden and caramelized, and slightly spicy thanks to the kick of crushed red pepper. They're so meaty and addictive, I could eat the entire bowl by myself.

* At least 4 hours ahead of time and up to the night before, soak einkorn berries in enough water to cover and add a teaspoon of apple cider vinegar. When ready to use, drain and rinse berries and place in a saucepan over medium heat with a cup (235 ml) of water. Bring mixture to a boil and reduce to a simmer, cooking until al dente, about 30 to 45 minutes. You'll know the berries are cooked when they are no longer hard, just slightly chewy. Remove from heat and strain any excess water.

* Meanwhile, warm a tablespoon (14 g) of coconut oil in a large saucepan and add sliced mushrooms, salt, pepper, and crushed red pepper. Cook, stirring often, until mushrooms are soft and shiny, about 20 to 30 minutes.

* In a medium-size bowl, combine cooked berries, mushrooms, and parsley. Serve warm, with grated Pecorino cheese as a garnish.

Yield: 4 servings

1 cup (200 g) einkorn berries

1 teaspoon apple cider vinegar

1 cup (235 ml) water

1 tablespoon (14 g) coconut oil

½ pound (8 ounces, or 225 g) mushrooms, sliced

½ teaspoon sea salt

½ teaspoon black pepper

½ teaspoon crushed red pepper

¼ cup (5 g) chopped parsley

Grated Pecorino cheese, for garnish

HERBED TOMATO SALAD

*N*ot only is this herby tomato salad a great seasonal side dish on its own, but it's also the perfect filling for Stuffed Tomatoes (page 134). Rich in pure tomato flavor and filled with fresh herbs, it's a creamy, savory option for a summer salad.

* At least 8 hours and up to a day or two beforehand, set einkorn berries in a bowl and cover with water, adding apple cider vinegar and covering on the counter. Check periodically to make sure it's not out of water (if so, add more). If you soak for longer than a day, drain, rinse, and refresh the water every 24 hours. The longer you let the berries sit, the more they will sprout and become easier to digest in the process.

* When ready to use the berries, drain the water, rinse the berries, and add them to a pot on the stove. Cover with stock or water and bring mixture to a boil. Then, reduce to a simmer, cover the pot, and let cook until water is absorbed and berries are cooked, about 30 minutes. Drain berries.

* In a large skillet, warm a tablespoon (15 ml) of olive oil and add chopped onion. Sauté until translucent, adding salt and pepper along the way. Add cooked, drained einkorn berries to the pan and stir. Add chopped, drained tomatoes (either reserve liquid for another use or discard). Add fresh herbs, stir, and add salt and pepper to taste.

*Yield: 3 to 4
servings as a side dish*

1 cup (200 g) einkorn berries

1 teaspoon apple cider vinegar

1 cup (235 ml) chicken, vegetable, or beef stock (or water)

1 tablespoon (15 ml) olive oil, plus more for drizzling on tomatoes before baking

½ onion, chopped

¼ teaspoon sea salt

¼ teaspoon black pepper

10 medium tomatoes, chopped and drained over a strainer

¾ cup (12 g) roughly torn fresh basil (from about 20 leaves)

5 sprigs parsley, chopped

4 sprigs thyme, chopped

ITALIAN-STYLE KALE AND EINKORN BERRY SALAD

Ever since my friend Ashley told me about the cheesy, bread crumb–filled Tuscan Kale Salad recipe on the blog 101 Cookbooks, it's been a staple in our home. This riff on that Italian classic adds einkorn berries to the mix, creating a much more filling, but still savory and delicious, side dish. Also, once everything's tossed and massaged, the small, pale berries and bread crumbs blend together so well, it's hard to tell which is which.

* In a large bowl, combine kale, bread crumbs, einkorn berries, and Pecorino. In a separate small bowl, whisk together olive oil, lemon juice, garlic, and salt. Pour about half of this dressing over the kale mixture, and use clean hands to massage everything together. Taste and add more dressing to taste.

Yield: 4 servings

FOR THE SALAD:

4 cups (75 g) chopped kale

⅔ cup (78 g) Herbed Bread Crumbs (page 70)

½ cup (95 g) Cooked Einkorn Berries (page 15)

½ cup (50 g) grated Pecorino cheese

FOR THE DRESSING:

¼ cup (60 ml) olive oil

¼ cup (60 g) lemon juice

1 clove of garlic, grated

½ teaspoon sea salt

Recipe Note

• *For another twist on this recipe, try doubling and roasting the garlic in the dressing, mashing it instead of grating.*

PARSLEY PESTO CAPRESE SALAD

This bright pesto salad pairs chewy einkorn berries with the classic, bold flavors of a caprese salad. Versatile enough to be eaten on its own or atop toast, it's an excellent starter, side dish, or basic salad. We're especially partial to containers of it packed away for road trips or lunches on the go.

* In a food processor or high-powered blender, combine minced garlic, chopped parsley, Pecorino, olive oil, pine nuts, and salt. Blend until thick and smooth.

* In a large bowl, combine the Pesto sauce with einkorn berries, diced tomatoes, and diced mozzarella. Toss together with a big spoon; taste, and adjust salt as needed. Serve immediately!

Yield: 4 servings

FOR THE PESTO:

4 cloves of garlic, minced

½ cup (30 g) chopped parsley

½ cup (50 g) grated Pecorino

½ cup (120 ml) olive oil

½ cup (68 g) pine nuts

¼ teaspoon coarse salt

FOR THE SALAD:

2 cups (380 g) Cooked Einkorn Berries (page 15)

2 Roma tomatoes, diced

8 ounces (226 g) fresh mozzarella, diced

CLASSIC PANZANELLA

Growing up, either one of us would have told you pizza was our favorite food—but that was probably because we hadn't yet had panzanella. Filled with bright, fresh flavors that soak into the dry bread cubes, panzanella is as easy to make as it is addictive. We could eat it every day.

* Place the tomatoes, onion, cucumber, basil, and bread cubes in a large 4-quart (4 L) mixing bowl, and toss everything together with a big spoon.

* Add olive oil, balsamic vinegar, and salt; toss together again. Taste, and adjust as you like.

* To serve, transfer salad to smaller 2-quart (2 L) bowl, if desired.

Yield: 2 to 4 servings

2 cups (335 g) chopped ripe tomatoes

¼ cup (30 g) chopped white or yellow onion

¼ cup (35 g) peeled, sliced cucumber

¾ cup (12 g) roughly torn fresh basil (from about 20 leaves)

2½ to 3 cups (135 g) toasted, cubed einkorn sourdough bread (pages 66 and 68)

¼ cup (60 ml) olive oil

2 tablespoons (30 ml) balsamic vinegar

½ teaspoon sea salt

Recipe Note

• *In order to minimize messes, we find it easiest to mix the bulky ingredients in panzanellas in larger-than-needed bowls. As you stir and combine the ingredients, the crusty bread soaks up the liquids and decreases in size, making it easier to transfer to a smaller serving bowl or platter.*

RADISH PANZANELLA

When we make this panzanella, it's not at all uncommon to find one of us sitting on the sofa with an entire bowl of it in our lap. Bright with parsley, tangy with lemon, it's a fresh, delightful way to redeem old bread.

✳ Place all the ingredients in a large, 4-quart (4 L) bowl, and toss everything together with spoons or your clean hands. Keep working the mixture together until everything is well coated. Cover with a towel and let rest at room temperature for 15 minutes, so the bread can soak up the salad juices. Taste; adjust as you like with more oil, salt, lemon juice, and so on. Transfer to a serving bowl or platter and serve.

Yield: 4 cups, or 2 to 4 servings

1 cup (110 g) thinly sliced radishes (from about 10 radishes)

1 cup (120 g) diced onion

½ cup (40 g) chopped radish greens

¼ cup (7 g) chopped parsley

¼ cup (50 g) diced tomato

2 tablespoons (30 ml) lemon juice

1 tablespoon (15 ml) olive oil

½ teaspoon sea salt

2½ to 3 cups (140 g) toasted, cubed sourdough bread (page 66 or 68)

Recipe Note

• *In order to minimize messes, we find it easiest to mix the bulky ingredients in panzanellas in larger-than-needed bowls. As you stir and combine the ingredients, the crusty bread soaks up the liquids and decreases in size, making it easier to transfer to a smaller serving bowl or platter.*

CORN AND WHITE BEAN SALAD

The sweetness of the corn beautifully balances the heartiness of the beans in this delicious salad. This recipe makes a wonderful lunch with some crusty bread on the side, or it works well as a side dish for dinner.

* In a medium stockpot over medium heat, cover the beans with water and bring to a boil. Reduce heat to a simmer and cook for about 2 hours, until beans are al dente, adding more water as needed as it evaporates. When you cook the beans uncovered, they won't get super soft, but they'll achieve a firm texture that holds up well in salads. (Another option, to speed the process, is to cook the beans in a covered pot, for about 1 to 1½ hours, which will yield much softer beans.)

* In a separate pot, combine berries with enough water to cover, and bring mixture to a boil. Reduce to a simmer, cooking until al dente, about 30 to 45 minutes. You'll know the berries are cooked when they are no longer hard, just slightly chewy. Remove from heat and strain any excess water.

* In a large sauté pan, add garlic and butter, and cook over medium-low heat until garlic is soft, fragrant, and beginning to brown. Add corn and the 2 tablespoons (30 ml) of water. Continue to cook over medium-low heat until corn is hot throughout, but still firm, about 5 to 10 minutes. Remove from heat, straining any excess water, and add to the bowl of einkorn berries.

* Add the chopped parsley to the bowl of einkorn mixture, and toss well to combine. Drain the cooked beans, add them to the bowl, and toss. Drizzle olive oil and lemon juice on the salad, season to taste with sea salt and pepper, and then mix again. Serve at room temperature.

Yield: 4 to 6 servings

1 cup (195 g) cannellini or great northern beans, soaked overnight and drained

½ cup (100 g) einkorn berries, soaked overnight and drained

4 to 6 cloves garlic, quartered

1 tablespoon (14 g) butter

2½ cups (325 g) frozen organic corn

2 tablespoons (30 ml) water

½ cup (30 g) chopped parsley

2 to 3 tablespoons (30 to 45 ml) olive oil

2 to 3 teaspoons fresh-squeezed lemon juice

Sea salt and black pepper, to taste

MEDITERRANEAN SALAD

This satisfying vegetarian salad pairs einkorn berries with Mediterranean favorites such as Peppadew peppers, olives, olive oil, and lemon juice for the sort of lunch that carries you well through to dinner.

* In a large bowl, combine cooked berries, spinach, peppers, goat cheese, and olives. In a separate, small bowl, whisk together vinegar, honey, lemon juice, olive oil, salt, and pepper. Drizzle this dressing over the berry mixture and toss to coat everything evenly. Taste; adjust salt and pepper as you like.

Yield: 4 servings

1½ cups (275 g) Cooked Einkorn Berries (page 15)

1 cup (30 to 35 g) chopped spinach

2 to 3 Peppadew peppers, diced

1 ounce (28 g) goat cheese

¼ cup chopped green Italian olives (such as Cerignola or Castelvetrano)

¼ cup (60 ml) balsamic vinegar

1 tablespoon (20 g) honey

2 tablespoons (30 ml) fresh lemon juice

1 to 2 tablespoons (15 to 30 ml) olive oil

¼ teaspoon sea salt

¼ teaspoon black pepper

Recipe Notes

• Although Peppadew peppers actually originate in South Africa, they pair so beautifully with olives and lemon juice that we love them in this Mediterranean side dish.

• If you can't find Peppadew peppers at your local grocery store, try Peppadew.com.

DRIED FRUIT AND TOASTED ALMOND EINKORN BERRY SALAD

At a family party a few years ago, someone served a version of this salad with quinoa and different dried fruits and nuts, and we liked that combination so much, we had to recreate it at home. In this einkorn version, we pair cooked berries with toasted almonds, diced bell pepper, dates, raisins, basil, and a bright vinaigrette for the sort of party salad everyone will remember.

✳ At least 4 hours ahead of time and up to the night before, soak einkorn berries in enough water to cover and add apple cider vinegar. When ready to use, drain and rinse. Set einkorn berries in a saucepan with a cup (235 ml) of water, and bring to a boil over medium heat. Reduce to a simmer, cover, and cook for 30 to 45 minutes, until berries are no longer hard, but only slightly chewy. Drain any excess water.

✳ While einkorn berries are cooking, prepare dressing in a small bowl: Whisk together olive oil, lemon juice, Dijon mustard, salt, pepper, and cumin. When berries are done, combine them in a large bowl with almonds, red pepper, dates, raisins, and basil. Drizzle some of the dressing on top of the salad, and toss well to combine; taste and add more salt, cumin, and/or dressing as needed. Any leftover dressing may be reserved and stored in the fridge for other use, such as adding a bright, fresh flavor to other salads.

Yield: 4 to 6 servings

FOR THE SALAD:

1 cup (200 g) einkorn berries

1 teaspoon apple cider vinegar

1 cup (235 ml) water

⅓ cup (37 g) blanched slivered almonds, toasted

1½ cups (220 g) diced red bell pepper (from 1 red bell pepper)

6 dried dates, chopped

6 tablespoons (180 g) raisins

2 tablespoons (4 g) torn fresh basil

FOR THE DRESSING:

½ cup (120 ml) olive oil

⅛ to ¼ cup (30 to 60 ml) fresh lemon juice

½ teaspoon Dijon mustard

¼ teaspoon sea salt, plus more to taste

¼ teaspoon pepper

⅛ to ¼ teaspoon cumin

Recipe Note

• *If you're not planning to eat all the salad at once, only add the toasted almonds when serving. Leftover salad keeps well in the fridge for about a week, but the almonds tend to lose their crunch over time.*

BUTTERNUT SQUASH PILAF

This savory pilaf capitalizes on the texture of creamy cooked einkorn berries by combining them with similarly creamy butternut squash purée. Toasted pine nuts add crunch, chopped parsley adds brightness, and the combination becomes a warm salad or side dish with a strong squash appeal.

* Preheat oven to 375°F (190°C, or gas mark 5) and grease or line a rimmed baking sheet with parchment.

* Cut squash in half vertically and scoop out seeds. Place squash halves on prepared baking sheet. Rub lightly with coconut oil.

* Roast squash, cut-side-down, for 45 minutes, until soft. Let cool.

* Scoop flesh into food processor and purée until smooth.

* In a large bowl, combine ½ cup (122 g) roasted squash purée with remaining ingredients, tossing everything to coat well. Adjust salt to taste. Serve warm.

Yield: 2 to 3 servings

1 butternut squash

1 to 2 tablespoons (15 to 30 ml) coconut oil

1 cup (250 g) Cooked Einkorn Berries (page 15)

¼ cup (35 g) pine nuts, toasted

¼ cup (10 g) chopped parsley

½ teaspoon sea salt

Recipe Note

• *Leftover squash purée may be covered and refrigerated for later use. It should keep for up to a week in the fridge..*

CHAPTER 6

Main Dishes

Sharing a meal represents sharing life. We tell our stories and listen to one another's while passing serving bowls and plates. That's what we love most about cooking and eating together, and that's what we love the most about this chapter.

The truth is, there's more to whole grains than desserts and side dishes, despite what you might think. From einkorn risotto (using berries in lieu of rice) to hearty einkorn-studded stews, the time-honored einkorn berry can pack a powerful punch in terms of satisfying food.

❖ Kale and Red Pepper Risotto ..104

❖ Red Wine Risotto 107

❖ Meat and Potato Pasties 108

❖ Italian Meatball
  Sandwiches 110

❖ Spicy Salmon over Cilantro
  Lime Einkorn 111

❖ California-Style BLT with
  Roasted Garlic and Rosemary
  Yogurt Sauce 112

❖ Breaded Lemon Chicken
  with Capers on Pilaf 114

❖ Kale and Cremini Vegetable
  Pot Pie 117

❖ Vegetable Lentil Stew 118

❖ Vegetable Soup with
  Red Wine and Lemon 121

❖ Italian-Style Mustard
  Green Soup 122

❖ Lamb-Stuffed Peppers 123

❖ Whole-Grain Egg Noodles 124

❖ Thai Noodle Bowls 125

❖ Basic Pasta Dough 126

❖ Ravioli with Sundried Tomatoes,
  Capers, and Ricotta 127

❖ Butternut Squash Gnocchi
  with Sweet Garlic–Ginger
  Brown Butter Sauce 128

❖ Thin and Crispy Pizza
  Crust 130

❖ Strawberry Leek Pizza
  with Kefir Crust 130

❖ Sourdough Pizza Crust 133

❖ Parsley Pesto Pizza 133

❖ Stuffed Tomatoes 134

RED WINE RISOTTO

The first time we made einkorn risotto was a revelation: "You mean you can use einkorn berries instead of rice?" While what results is a slightly chewier version of the old Italian classic, it is every bit as creamy and comforting—a refined, satisfying favorite.

* At least 4 hours ahead of time and up to the night before, soak einkorn berries in enough water to cover and add a teaspoon of apple cider vinegar. When ready to use, drain and rinse and set aside.

* Place the stock in a medium-size saucepan and heat until warm. While the stock is warming, place a large stockpot over medium heat and melt 2 tablespoons (28 g) butter. Add sliced onions to the butter and cook until onions are translucent, stirring occasionally, about 10 minutes.

* Add einkorn berries to onions and stir everything together until coated. Add wine and 1 cup (235 ml) of warm stock. Cook risotto at a low simmer, stirring constantly, until most of the liquid is absorbed; when you push a section of the berries down, liquid should not immediately refill the space. Add another ½ cup (120 ml) stock and cook/stir until absorbed. Repeat this process until all the stock has been used, which will take about 45 minutes. Once done, the grains should be soft and plump but more al dente in doneness than rice (if they are still hard, add more broth and keep cooking).

* Add the remaining 2 tablespoons (28 g) butter, fresh thyme, and grated Pecorino cheese. Add salt and pepper to taste, and garnish with a big squeeze of lemon and extra cheese and thyme if desired.

Yield: 1 quart (4 cups, or 660 g) risotto, or 4 servings

1 cup (200 g) of einkorn berries

1 teaspoon apple cider vinegar

4 to 4½ cups (940 ml to 1 L) vegetable, chicken, or beef stock

4 tablespoons (55 g) butter, divided

½ cup to 1 cup (115 g) sliced onion

¼ cup (60 ml) red wine (such as Cabernet Sauvignon)

2 teaspoons fresh thyme, plus more for garnish (or 1 teaspoon dried thyme)

¼ cup (25 g) grated Pecorino cheese, plus more for garnish

Sea salt and black pepper, to taste

Lemon wedges, for garnish

KALE AND RED PEPPER RISOTTO

If you ask Tim about his favorite kind of food, he'll say "peasant-style Italian," which basically means recipes like this one, despite what the term *risotto* might make you think. While it's true risotto today is associated with fancy restaurants and impressive menus, in actuality, it's an incredibly simple, comforting dish. This kale and red pepper version bursts with rich flavor in every bite, from the einkorn berries plumped up with stock to the sautéed vegetables surrounding them.

* At least 4 hours ahead of time and up to the night before, soak einkorn berries in enough water to cover and add a teaspoon of apple cider vinegar. When ready to use, drain and rinse.

* In a saucepan, warm 4 cups (950 ml) of stock over medium heat and keep at a simmer. In a large stockpot, warm 3 tablespoons (42 g) butter. Add einkorn berries and toast them in the butter over medium heat for about 10 minutes, stirring frequently. Add ½ cup (120 ml) of stock and continue cooking, stirring frequently, until stock is absorbed and liquid doesn't immediately refill a section when you push at it with a spoon. Repeat this process with the einkorn berries, adding ½ cup (120 ml) of stock at a time and stirring until it absorbs, until all the stock has been incorporated, about an hour.

* In between cooking einkorn berries, set a large skillet on an adjacent burner and warm a tablespoon (14 g) of coconut oil over medium heat. Add sliced onion, chopped peppers, salt, and pepper, and cook until softened, about 10 to 15 minutes. Add chopped kale and stir/cook until it wilts, about 5 minutes. Remove from heat.

* Add kale-pepper-onion mixture and grated Pecorino cheese to pot of einkorn berries and stir everything together. Taste and adjust for salt. Serve in bowls, with freshly grated cheese.

Yield: 1 quart (4 cups, or 660 g) risotto, or 4 servings

1 cup (200 g) einkorn berries

1 teaspoon apple cider vinegar

4 cups (950 ml) vegetable, beef, or chicken stock

3 tablespoons (42 g) butter

1 tablespoon (14 g) coconut oil

½ medium (100 g) onion, sliced

½ large (150 g) red pepper, seeds removed and diced

½ teaspoon sea salt

½ teaspoon black pepper

8 cups (125 g) roughly chopped kale, from half a bunch of kale with stems removed

½ cup (50 g) grated Pecorino cheese

MEAT AND POTATO PASTIES

I spent 3 years of college in northern Wisconsin, where meat pasties are not hard to find. From small shops to large diners, ground beef and potatoes are encased in buttery dough like large hand pies everywhere you look, perhaps to thicken everybody up for the long winters. In this recipe, we have a throwback to that comforting classic.

* Preheat oven to 350°F (180°C, or gas mark 4). In a medium bowl, combine einkorn flour and salt. Cut in butter with a pastry cutter until butter is in chunks throughout. Stir in 2 tablespoons (30 ml) of water, and stir until it begins to come together. If dough seems too crumbly and dry still, add up to 2 more tablespoons (30 ml) of water; if too wet, add a bit more flour. Use clean hands to form mixture into a solid ball of dough, pushing and forming the dough right in the bowl. Separate ball into 4 equal pieces, form them into balls, and place them in the fridge to rest and chill while you make the filling.

* In a large skillet over medium heat, melt coconut oil. Stir in onion, carrots, bell peppers, ¼ teaspoon salt, and pepper. Once everything's soft and golden, about 10 to 15 minutes, add potatoes and ground beef, along with the remaining salt and thyme. Stir mixture together and cook just long enough to lightly sear meat, a few minutes. Remove from heat.

* Working with 1 of the 4 rounds of dough at a time on floured parchment, use a floured rolling pin to create a 7 to 8-inch (18 to 20 cm) round. Place a few spoonfuls of the meat and vegetable mixture in the center, and pull the edges of the dough over the top, starting with the long sides and then sealing things together with the short sides. Place these pasties on a parchment-lined rimmed baking pan or sheet. Use a fork to press the edges, brush all 4 pasties with yogurt, and pierce all over with a fork. Leftover filling may be sautéed and eaten on its own, added to morning egg scrambles, added to pizzas, or frozen for later use.

* Bake in the oven for 60 to 75 minutes, until golden and firm.

Yield: 4 pasties

FOR THE DOUGH:

1¼ cups (156 g) all-purpose einkorn flour, plus more for working with the dough

½ teaspoon salt

½ cup (112 g) unsalted butter, cold and cubed

2 tablespoons to ¼ cup (30 ml to 60 ml) cold water

FOR THE FILLING:

1 tablespoon (13 g) coconut oil

¾ cup (90 g) chopped onion (about ½ onion)

¾ cup (90 g) chopped carrots (about 3 to 4 peeled carrots)

¾ cup (90 g) chopped bell peppers (about 1 bell pepper)

¾ teaspoon sea salt, divided

½ teaspoon pepper

¾ cup (90 g) chopped Yukon gold potatoes (about 1 potato)

¾ pound ground beef, preferably grass-fed

Leaves of 6 to 7 springs of thyme (or 1 tablespoon [4 g] dried thyme)

2 tablespoons (30 g) yogurt, for brushing

ITALIAN MEATBALL SANDWICHES

You don't have to use einkorn bread crumbs or einkorn bread to make Italian meatball sandwiches like these, but this recipe demonstrates yet again the versatility of this ancient grain. Here, the herbed einkorn bread crumbs (page 70) add lightness and softness to the baked and browned meatballs, and soft slices of einkorn sandwich bread (page 45) are perfect for creating filling, meaty, sauce-covered sandwiches everyone will enjoy. The 4-ingredient tomato sauce in this recipe is simple Italian food at its finest and one of our favorite ways to make sauce, originally inspired by legendary cook Marcella Hazan.

❊ For the sauce: In a large stockpot over medium heat, combine tomatoes, onions, and butter. Simmer for 45 minutes. Taste and adjust by adding sea salt as desired. Remove onions (you can freeze for making stock, use for another recipe, compost, or discard).

❊ For the meat: In a large bowl, combine beef, garlic, basil, parsley, Pecorino, sea salt, and pepper. Stir gently and break up beef to incorporate. Stir in eggs and then bread crumbs. Finally, add the milk. The mixture should not be too runny and should be able to hold form. Form meatballs by hand into 2½-inch (6 cm)-size balls and place onto rimmed baking sheet (no need to grease it—there is enough fat for the meatballs to brown on the bottom while baking). Bake at 375°F (190°C, or gas mark 5) for 35 minutes, turning meatballs in the pan once halfway through. After meatballs are browned, add meatballs and any pan juices to the sauce and simmer in sauce for at least 20 to 30 minutes, or longer to develop more flavor.

❊ For serving: Slice meatballs in half or thirds and place on toasted einkorn bread. Cover in sauce and grate extra Pecorino on top. Cover with another slice of toasted bread to serve.

Yield: About 19 sandwiches

FOR THE SAUCE:

26¼ ounces (750 g) crushed tomatoes (such as boxed San Marzano)

3 onions, peeled and halved

7 tablespoons (100 g) butter

Sea salt

FOR THE MEATBALLS:

2 pounds (900 g) ground beef, preferably grass-fed

3 to 4 cloves garlic, diced

¼ cup (4 g) chopped basil

¼ cup (15 g) chopped parsley (packed)

¾ cup (75 g) grated Pecorino cheese, plus more for serving

2 teaspoons sea salt

1 teaspoon black pepper

2 eggs

½ cup (55 g) Herbed Bread Crumbs (page 70)

3 tablespoons (45 ml) whole milk

FOR SERVING:

1 to 2 Soft Sandwich Loaves (page 45), sliced

SPICY SALMON OVER CILANTRO LIME EINKORN

*N*estled on a bed of bright and flavorful cilantro lime einkorn, this tender salmon is sweet and spicy, drizzled with what's similar to a homemade barbecue sauce.

* Preheat oven to 400°F (200°C, or gas mark 6). In a saucepan over medium heat, melt ghee. Add ginger powder and grated garlic, letting them toast in the ghee for a few minutes, until fragrant but not browned. Stir in salsa, sriracha, soy sauce, and sugar, and lower the heat to medium-low; cook this mixture for 3 to 5 minutes, until sugar dissolves and sauce is bubbly. Remove from heat.

* Combine pilaf ingredients in a medium bowl. Toss well to incorporate. Adjust salt to taste.

* Brush the top and bottom of the salmon filets with ghee, and place them in a small oven-safe dish. Sprinkle with salt and pepper on top. Bake for 10 to 15 minutes, until cooked through, but not dried out; insert a knife in the middle to check that it's done. Immediately pour sauce on top and serve hot on top of pilaf.

Yield: 2 to 4 servings

FOR THE SAUCE:

1 teaspoon ghee

¼ teaspoon ginger powder

1 clove garlic, grated

½ cup (120 g) tomato salsa (whatever heat level you prefer, we used medium)

¼ teaspoon sriracha

2 teaspoons organic soy sauce

2 tablespoons (26 g) of Sucanat or coconut sugar

FOR THE PILAF:

2¼ cups (428 g) Cooked Einkorn Berries (page 15)

¼ cup (12 g) chopped cilantro

2 tablespoons (30 ml) fresh lime juice

¼ teaspoon smoked red paprika

½ teaspoon sea salt

FOR THE SALMON:

1 pound (450 g) fresh wild-caught salmon fillets

2 teaspoons ghee

¼ teaspoon sea salt

⅛ teaspoon black pepper, optional

CALIFORNIA-STYLE BLT WITH ROASTED GARLIC AND ROSEMARY YOGURT SAUCE

Yield: 2 sandwiches

6 to 8 slices beef bacon

1 clove garlic

⅓ cup (77 g) yogurt

¾ teaspoon finely diced rosemary

¼ teaspoon black pepper

¼ teaspoon sea salt

4 slices Marble Rye Bread (page 49), toasted

2 leaves romaine lettuce

1 tomato, sliced

½ avocado, sliced

This recipe is one of our favorite ways to use the beautiful marble rye bread found on page 49. For the sandwich, toasted bread gets topped with bacon, avocado, tomato, lettuce, and a homemade garlicky yogurt sauce with bursts of rosemary for a refined take on the classic BLT. While we prefer beef or turkey bacon, you can swap in whatever type you like best.

✳ Preheat oven to 375°F (190°C, or gas mark 5). Place the bacon on a baking sheet and bake for 10 to 12 minutes, until crispy and brown. Add the garlic clove to the pan for the last 3 to 4 minutes, so it can roast in the juices. Once done, drain bacon and set aside.

✳ To make the yogurt sauce: In a small bowl mix roasted garlic clove, yogurt, rosemary, pepper, and sea salt. The roasted garlic should be soft enough to mash into the yogurt.

✳ To assemble the sandwich: On each slice of toasted rye, spread some of the rosemary yogurt. Then layer lettuce, 2 slices of bacon, tomato, 2 slices of bacon, avocado, and lettuce. Top with additional slice of bread.

Recipe Note

◆ *Save your bacon grease! It comes in handy for our Spinach Skillet Cornbread on page 52.*

BREADED LEMON CHICKEN WITH CAPERS ON PILAF

This recipe is straight out of my childhood, when my mom cooked chicken most nights. When it's cooking, it fills the kitchen with the scents of lemon, onion, and savory meat; once ready, it offers tender meat in creamy gravy studded with capers and lemon.

* Preheat oven to 375°F (190°C, or gas mark 5). Pound chicken breasts to be about ½ inch (13 mm) thick, and sprinkle salt and pepper on each side. Mix together flour, garlic powder, and paprika in a rimmed plate. Mix together egg and Pecorino in a separate rimmed plate. Warm a stainless steel pan over medium heat and melt a tablespoon (13 g) of coconut oil inside. Dredge chicken breasts in flour mixture, then egg mixture, then sauté in pan on each side (no need to redip in flour), just long enough to sear and brown, 3 to 4 minutes. Remove chicken to an 8-inch (20 cm) baking pan.

* To the same pan you just cooked the chicken in, melt 1 tablespoon (14 g) of butter. Add onion and garlic, cooking until translucent and fragrant, scraping the pan with a metal spatula to scoop up breading in pan. After 5 to 10 minutes, add broth; the pan will steam and sizzle and it will be a little scary, but 2 seconds later you'll be fine. Mix together a tablespoon (8 g) of flour and a tablespoon (15 ml) of water in a bowl; add it and 2 tablespoons (28 g) of butter to pan. Reduce for 15 minutes. Meanwhile, add lemon slices and capers to the chicken dish. Pour broth mixture over the chicken, and bake 30 to 40 minutes, until fully cooked, with a thick sauce and tender meat.

* While chicken cooks, prepare pilaf by combining cooked berries and Pecorino in a small saucepan over lowest possible heat. Serve chicken pieces atop ¼-cup (55 g) piles of einkorn pilaf, spooning pan juices over top.

Yield: 2 to 4 servings

FOR THE BREADED LEMON CHICKEN:

2 boneless, skinless chicken breasts (about a pound)

1 teaspoon sea salt

1 teaspoon black pepper

½ cup (63 g) all-purpose einkorn flour, plus a tablespoon (8 g) for sauce

½ teaspoon garlic powder

½ teaspoon smoked red paprika

1 egg

¼ cup (25 g) grated Pecorino cheese

1 tablespoon (13 g) coconut oil

3 tablespoons (42 g) butter, divided

½ onion (80 to 100 g), sliced

1 clove of garlic, grated

1 cup (235 ml) broth

1 tablespoon (15 ml) water

½ lemon, sliced into 6 to 8 slices

2 tablespoons (17 g) capers

FOR THE PILAF:

1 cup (190 g) Cooked Einkorn Berries (page 15)

1 tablespoon (6 g) grated Pecorino

KALE AND CREMINI VEGETABLE POT PIE

In this vegetarian spin on pot pie, a rich and hearty turmeric-colored stew of vegetables and spices cooks beneath a flaky, buttery pie crust topping. Sliced and served in bowls or on plates, each sloppy piece is the definition of comfort food: hot, creamy, and delicious.

* Warm coconut oil in a 3- or 4-quart (3 or 4 L) stockpot over medium heat. Add diced carrots, onion, mushrooms, coriander, chili powder, and turmeric powder, and stir together to coat everything evenly with oil and spices. Let this mixture cook for 10 to 15 minutes, until onions are translucent. Add kale and toss to coat; cook until kale wilts and reduces dramatically in size. Add stock. Taste mixture and add salt and pepper to taste (amount will vary based on type and saltiness of stock). Remove pot from heat and add milk and flour.

* Preheat oven to 350°F (180°C, or gas mark 4). Pour vegetable mixture into a 9-inch (23 cm) pie plate (if you have excess leftover, it may be warmed on the stove and eaten as soup).

* Top with the prepared pie crust, forming and cutting it around the edges in order to fit the plate. Slash the top in the middle, to allow air to escape while the pie bakes. Brush the top of the dough with milk.

* Bake for 45 to 50 minutes, until crust is golden. Let cool slightly before slicing. Serve warm.

Yield: 6 to 8 servings

FOR THE VEGETABLE FILLING:

1 tablespoon (13 g) coconut oil

4 carrots, peeled and diced

1 large onion, peeled and diced

8 baby bella cremini mushrooms, sliced

1 teaspoon coriander

1 teaspoon chili powder

½ teaspoon turmeric powder

1 bunch of kale, roughly chopped

1½ cups (12 ounces) vegetable or chicken stock

Generous sea salt and black pepper to taste

½ cup (120 ml) milk, plus more for brushing pie crust

2 tablespoons (16 g) all-purpose flour

FOR THE PIE CRUST:

Pie crust dough (page 156), rolled out onto floured surface

VEGETABLE LENTIL STEW

There's nothing better on a cold night than a pot of hot soup on the stove. This thick and chunky stew combines firm and nutty French lentils with plumped einkorn berries and cooked vegetables for a soothing, filling soup that warms you right up.

* At least 8 hours ahead of time and up to overnight, place the einkorn berries in a bowl with enough water to cover and the apple cider vinegar. Place the French lentils in a separate bowl with enough water to cover. Cover both bowls with a towel.

* After letting berries and lentils soak, strain liquid, rinse, and place the berries and lentils in a large 4-quart (4 L) stock pot. Cover with water and bring to a boil. Reduce heat to simmer and cook for about an hour, until lentils are tender.

* Meanwhile, in a large skillet, warm coconut oil over medium heat. Add carrots, peppers, white onions, and red onions. Toss to coat everything with oil, and add salt and pepper. Cook until softened, but not caramelized, about 10 minutes. Add greens and toss, cooking until just barely wilted. Remove pan from heat.

* When berries and lentils are done cooking, add all the vegetable mixture to the pot, along with enough water to cover. Cook for another 20 minutes, or until all the vegetables are softened. Season with additional salt and pepper to taste.

Yield: 8 to 10 servings

1 cup (200 g) einkorn berries

1 teaspoon apple cider vinegar

1 cup (192 g) French lentils

1 tablespoon (13 g) coconut oil

4 large carrots, peeled and diced

1 cup (150 g) chopped bell pepper (about 3 mini, seeded bell peppers)

1 white onion, sliced

½ red onion, sliced

1 teaspoon sea salt

½ teaspoon black pepper

¼ to ⅓ cup (5 to 7 g) chopped greens (spinach, kale, chard, radish greens, etc.)

VEGETABLE SOUP WITH RED WINE AND LEMON

The beauty of a soup like this one, which as written is packed with winter vegetables, is that it's highly adaptable. In spring, substitute peas and red radishes for the peppers and daikon radishes. In fall, swap in chopped squash. The constants are sautéed vegetables, a hefty dose of stock, red wine, lemon juice, and greens—as long as those elements remain, you have an easy, go-to recipe for a flavorful, comforting dinner.

* In a large 3- or 4-quart (3 or 4 L) stockpot over medium heat, melt coconut oil and add salt and pepper, letting it toast for a few seconds in the oil. Add chopped onion, chopped carrots, chopped peppers, chopped daikon radishes, chopped turnip, and minced garlic. Cook this mixture until onions are translucent and vegetables are soft, about 15 to 20 minutes. Add chopped parsley and cook 5 minutes more.

* Add broth, red wine, lemon juice, and kale, and stir together. Cook this mixture for an additional 20 minutes. Finally, add cooked einkorn berries, stir together, and let simmer for 15 minutes. Taste and adjust salt and pepper as needed. Serve in bowls, with bread on the side if desired.

Yield: 8 to 10 servings

1 tablespoon (13 g) coconut oil

1 teaspoon sea salt

1 teaspoon black pepper

1 large white or yellow onion, chopped

2 large carrots, chopped

2 small peppers, chopped

2 daikon radishes, chopped

1 small turnip, chopped

2 cloves garlic, minced

2 tablespoons (8 g) chopped parsley

4 cups (940 ml) unsalted vegetable, chicken, or beef broth

⅓ cup (80 ml) red wine

2 tablespoons (30 ml) lemon juice (half a lemon)

2 handfuls of kale (115 g), leaves torn from stems

1 cup (200 g) Cooked Einkorn Berries (page 15)

ITALIAN-STYLE MUSTARD GREEN SOUP

Mustard greens are known for their hot and spicy taste, but cooking them with garlic and olive oil in a soup helps to tame that powerful kick. Here, combined with the einkorn berries, the greens make a classic Italian soup that makes us think of Tim's grandma, Emily, who frequently served him sautéed mustard greens in a broth of water, olive oil, and garlic. Note that if you cook the einkorn berries in the soup for a long time, they will get softer and eventually break open (or puff). Some people like it that way better, but either way is good. You may also cook them to al dente separately, then add to individual bowls of soup as desired. We love serving this soup with slices of One-Bowl Butter Bread (page 46).

* Soak berries in enough water to cover (with a splash of apple cider vinegar or lemon, if you have it) for 4 to 8 hours or overnight. In the morning, drain and rinse berries and set in a saucepan with a cup (235 ml) of water; bring to boil; reduce to simmer; cover, and cook for about 40 minutes until al dente (they will be firm and still chewy). Check on the berries periodically as they cook; if they're low on water, add another tablespoon or so, just enough to prevent burning.

* In a 3½-quart (3.5 L) stockpot over medium heat, sauté garlic and onions in olive oil until garlic is just beginning to brown. Add in mustard greens and sauté for another 1 to 2 minutes until the greens begin to wilt and are infused with the olive oil. Then add chicken broth and remaining water, bring to a boil, then reduce heat and simmer for 30 minutes. Add cooked einkorn berries and sea salt to taste.

* Serve with a drizzle of olive oil and freshly grated Pecorino or Parmiggiano cheese.

Yield: 2½ to 3 quarts (2½ to 3 L) soup, or 8 to 10 servings

¾ cup (150 g) einkorn berries

3 cups (475 ml) water, divided

2 cloves of garlic

1 cup (160 g) sliced onion

2 to 4 tablespoons (28 to 60 ml) olive oil

½ bunch (8 cups, or 145 g) mustard greens, stems removed and chopped

2 cups (475 ml) chicken broth

Sea salt to taste

Olive oil and grated Pecorino or Parmiggiano cheese, for serving

LAMB-STUFFED PEPPERS

$\mathcal{T}$he filling in these peppers is so tasty—a savory, meaty, tomato mixture studded with fresh mint—that we could eat it on its own. But stuffed into bell peppers, topped with cheese and bread crumbs, and baked until soft, it gets even better. We love making these peppers as a savory, special dinner treat.

✳ In a large (10-inch [25 cm]) skillet over medium heat, melt coconut oil. Once oil is hot, add onion and garlic, stirring them into the oil to coat. Let cook 5 to 10 minutes, until onion is translucent and beginning to turn golden. Add lamb, salt, and pepper, and use a wooden spoon to break up the meat and stir everything together. Let mixture cook for another 5 to 10 minutes, stirring often, until meat is browned and cooked through. Add strained tomatoes and cooked einkorn berries, lower heat to medium-low, and cook until most of the liquids are absorbed, about 15 minutes.

✳ While lamb mixture cooks, grease a pan big enough to hold your peppers (probably 8 x 8-inch [20 x 20 cm] but perhaps larger if you have wide peppers) with a little coconut oil. Preheat oven to 375°F (190°C, or gas mark 5). Use a sharp knife to cut a circle around the top of each pepper, around the stem, and pull it out and discard. Scoop out any seeds inside, keeping the pepper shape intact. Set these hollowed peppers in the prepared pan.

✳ Once liquids are mostly evaporated from the lamb pan, remove pan from heat and add grated Pecorino and mint. Scoop meat filling into the hollowed peppers, distributing evenly among them. Top peppers with bread crumbs and extra Pecorino.

✳ Bake peppers, uncovered, for 45 minutes to an hour, until peppers are no longer firm, but soft and easy to pierce with a fork. Serve immediately.

Yield: 4 to 6 servings

2 tablespoons (28 g) coconut oil, plus more for greasing pan

2 cups (260 g) chopped white onion (about 1 or 2 onions)

4 garlic cloves, grated

1 pound (450 g) ground lamb

1 teaspoon sea salt

1 teaspoon black pepper

1 cup (180 g) strained tomatoes (such as POMI brand)

1 cup (190 g) Cooked Einkorn Berries (page 15)

6 bell peppers

1 cup (100 g) grated Pecorino, plus more for garnish

¼ cup (24 g) chopped fresh mint, plus more for garnish

½ cup (55 g) Herbed Bread Crumbs (page 70)

WHOLE-GRAIN EGG NOODLES

We know what you're thinking: "Homemade einkorn noodles? Who has time for that?" Before you write this recipe off as too time-intensive, however, let us sell you on its charms. Watching dough transform into long, elastic strips is nothing short of magic, and everyone should experience a little magic now and then. What's more, once you feel comfortable with your pasta maker, whipping these noodles out is truly a breeze. Plus, the reward of eating a meal with the noodles you formed from scratch? That's pretty priceless.

* In a food processor, combine flour, salt, and eggs, pulsing for 30 to 60 seconds at a time. If mixture seems crumbly, add a tablespoon (15 ml) of water at a time and remix. If it seems wet and is sticking to the sides of the processor, add a tablespoon (7 g) of extra flour at a time and remix. When dough begins to come together into a ball, remove with floured hands and knead on a floured surface a few times. Set in a bowl to rest for 30 minutes.

* Divide rested dough into 4 equal portions. Following your pasta maker's instructions, work 1 section at a time into long, thin strips of dough adding extra flour to dough and surface whenever things get sticky. Using the noodle attachment, cut these strips into noodles and set them over rods or pans to dry. (We like to stick bamboo skewers under heavy books at the edge of our dining room table and lay the noodles on top of these to dry.) Noodles may be used immediately, or they may be dried for a few hours first. They also may be dried and frozen for later use.

*Yield: ½ pound (230 g)
noodles, or 2 to 4 servings*

2 cups (220 g) whole-grain einkorn flour, plus more for dusting surfaces

½ teaspoon sea salt

2 eggs

Water, if needed

Recipe Note

• *Noodles may be cooked and eaten immediately, dried for a few hours and cooked, or even formed into nests and frozen for later use.*

THAI NOODLE BOWLS

The idea for this recipe occurred late one night when we'd just returned from a trip and the kitchen pickings were slim. "I'm starving!" I said to Tim, and, within an hour, a version of this is what he brought me. We both liked it so much, we made it again a few nights later, only with homemade einkorn egg noodles—pure magic. Now, every time I think about these noodle bowls, I think about what a sweet man I married.

* In a large skillet over medium heat, warm 2 tablespoons (28 ml) of olive oil. Meanwhile, fill a 3- or 4-quart (3 or 4 L) stockpot with water and a pinch of salt, set over medium to high heat, and bring to a rolling boil.

* Add onion and nuts to the skillet, and stir everything together. Add spices (cinnamon, ginger, crushed red pepper, cumin, and sriracha) to the pan and stir again. Sauté for 5 to 10 minutes, then add the curry paste and balsamic vinegar, tossing to coat the onions and nuts. Sauté for 3 to 5 minutes more, then add the sweet red peppers.

* When the water in the stockpot comes to a boil, add the egg noodles and cook for 3 to 5 minutes, until al dente. If the pasta is fresh, it will cook extremely quickly; if it's dried a little while, it will take a few minutes longer. Reserve ¼ cup (60 ml) of the cooking liquid and strain remaining.

* Add the drained egg noodles to the skillet along with the reserved cooking liquid, stirring everything together to coat. Garnish with chopped parsley.

Yield: 2 to 4 servings

2 tablespoons (28 ml) olive oil

½ teaspoon sea salt

¾ cup (90 g) chopped onion

¼ cup (36 g) chopped almonds or peanuts (or other nut)

¼ teaspoon cinnamon

½ teaspoon ginger powder

½ teaspoon crushed red pepper

¼ teaspoon cumin powder

½ teaspoon sriracha

1 teaspoon Thai green curry paste (such as Thai Kitchen brand)

1 tablespoon (15 ml) balsamic vinegar

½ cup (38 g) chopped sweet red peppers

½ pound Whole-Grain Egg Noodles (page 124)

⅛ cup chopped parsley

BASIC PASTA DOUGH

Making homemade pasta is one of those intimidating kitchen tasks that a lot of people are afraid to try—but when you do it in a food processor, everything changes! This incredibly foolproof pasta recipe comes together in minutes and yields a beautifully pale yellow einkorn dough perfect for using in everything from spaghetti to ravioli.

To make this dough without a food processor, combine everything in a large bowl, first stirring and then using your hands to create a dough. Follow the rest of the instructions as written.

* In a food processor, combine 2 cups (250 g) of flour and salt. Pulse a few times to combine. Add the eggs, cracking them right on top of the flour mixture. Process the mixture for 30 to 60 seconds. Stop when the dough comes together into a rough ball.

* Take a look at the dough. If it's dry, add a little bit of water. If it's wet/sticky, enough to be smearing against the side, add more flour. Repeat until the dough comes together in the processor, moving from crumbles into a cohesive giant piece of dough.

* Remove dough from food processor to a floured surface, and knead it for about 5 minutes, pressing and pushing on it until it's smooth and elastic. It should not stick to your hands (if it does, add more flour), but it should not have noticeable flour pieces either. Dust the finished ball of dough with a little flour and place it in a bowl. Cover with a towel, and let mixture rest at room temperature for 30 minutes. Use in your favorite pasta recipe or as directed in einkorn ravioli (page 127).

*Yield: 1 pound (450 g)
pasta dough*

**2 to 3 cups (250 to 375 g)
all-purpose einkorn flour**

½ teaspoon sea salt

3 eggs

RAVIOLI WITH SUNDRIED TOMATOES, CAPERS, AND RICOTTA

*I*f there is anything einkorn is perfect for, it's homemade pasta. Here, we take the elastic einkorn pasta dough from page 126 and turn it into beautiful pillows stuffed with sundried tomatoes, capers, and ricotta.

To prepare pasta for later use, uncooked ravioli may be formed and then frozen on parchment. Once firm, move ravioli to plastic bags and leave in the freezer until desired use.

* In a medium skillet, drizzle a tablespoon (15 ml) of olive oil and warm it over medium heat. Add capers, sundried tomatoes, and onion; sauté until soft, about 10 to 15 minutes. Remove this mixture to a bowl and combine with balsamic vinegar and ricotta.

* Divide pasta dough into 4 equal parts, removing 1 from the refrigerator at a time. On a floured surface, stretch out and press the dough as thinly as possible. For best results, do this in a pasta maker. Use the ravioli attachment of the pasta maker or biscuit cutters on the counter to cut out ravioli shapes. Set them on floured parchment while you continue working with the dough. Once all 4 portions of dough have been transferred to the parchment, place a dollop of prepared filling at the center of every other ravioli piece, leaving a ⅛- to ¼-inch (3 to 6 mm) border around the sides. Brush the edges with water, and layer an empty ravioli piece atop each filled one. Press down the edges with a fork.

* In a large stockpot over medium heat, bring water to a rolling boil. Drop ravioli in water, cooking them in batches, as many as will fit in the pot at a time, for about 4 to 5 minutes per batch. Ravioli will float to the surface when cooked, but before removing all of them, take one out and taste it for doneness. Use a slotted spoon to remove cooked ravioli to plates, and repeat process until all ravioli are cooked. Serve immediately, with olive oil or your favorite pasta sauce on top.

Yield: 24 to 36 ravioli, depending on size, or enough for 4 servings

1 tablespoon (15 ml) olive oil

1½ tablespoons (13 g) capers

2 ounces (56 g) sundried tomatoes

1 small onion, diced

1 tablespoon (15 ml) balsamic vinegar

15 ounces (425 g) ricotta cheese

1 pound (450 g) Basic Pasta Dough (page 126)

BUTTERNUT SQUASH GNOCCHI WITH SWEET GARLIC-GINGER BROWN BUTTER SAUCE

*M*aking gnocchi is a meditative process, one that requires stopping and paying attention. We like saving it for weekend afternoons, especially weekend afternoons in fall and winter, when squash is at its peak. Here, gnocchi pairs beautifully with sweet and spicy sauce, featuring both the sharp kick of ginger and the nutty pleasure of browned butter.

* Preheat oven to 375°F (190°C, or gas mark 5). Cut butternut squash in half vertically, scoop out the seeds, and rub the insides with coconut oil. Place face down on baking sheet, and roast 35 minutes, until a fork easily pierces the skin. Remove the squash from the oven; scoop the flesh into a food processor; purée; and pour into a bowl. (This may be done ahead of time.)

* In a large bowl, stir together 1 cup (260 g) squash puree with 2⅓ cups (290 g) einkorn flour, nutmeg, salt, and pepper. If the mixture is too sticky to handle, add more flour until you can work with the dough, erring on the sticky rather than over-floured side. Using a spoon and then your floured fingers, work the mixture into a smooth ball of dough. Separate the ball into 4 equal pieces, and roll balls into 1-inch (2.5 cm)-thick logs on a floured surface.

* In a stockpot over medium heat, bring 3 quarts (3 L) of water and ½ teaspoon salt to a boil. While water heats, use a floured knife to cut 1-inch (2.5 cm) squares of gnocchi dough, pressing with a fork. Drop these pieces into the boiling water and cook 10 to 15 minutes. The gnocchi will rise to the surface a little before being done.

* Warm 4 tablespoons (55 g) of butter in a saucepan over medium heat until it almost browns. Add ginger, garlic, salt, and coconut sugar, and cook a few minutes, until the moment when it starts to smell almost burned. To serve, place the gnocchi on a dish, top with a few spoonfuls of the reserved butternut squash pureé, and spoon brown butter sauce on top.

Yield: About 45 gnocchi, or enough for 2 to 3 servings

FOR THE GNOCCHI:

1 medium (2- to 3-pound [900 to 1350 g]) butternut squash

1 tablespoon (13 g) coconut oil, melted

2⅓ to 3 cups (290 to 375 g) all-purpose einkorn flour, plus more for surfaces

¾ teaspoon nutmeg

½ teaspoon sea salt, plus more for water

¼ teaspoon black pepper

FOR THE SAUCE:

4 tablespoons (55 g) butter

½ teaspoon freshly grated ginger

1 clove of garlic, grated

¼ teaspoon salt

1 tablespoon (13 g) coconut sugar

THIN AND CRISPY PIZZA CRUST ➤

Blame our 1980s childhoods or our Italian heritages: We could eat pizza every day, especially this einkorn one with its crisp, crackery crust.

* In a medium bowl, stir together 2 cups (250 g) einkorn flour, olive oil, salt, yeast, and kefir. Stir in warm water, and then, using your hands, knead mixture in bowl until it forms a nice dough (you can add up to ¼ cup [60 ml] extra warm water or ½ cup [63 g] more flour if needed). Form into a ball, and place in an oiled bowl, rolling to coat. Cover and leave in a warm place for at least an hour.

* When ready to use, preheat oven to 475°F (250°C, or gas mark 9). Split the dough in half, and stretch and roll each half onto parchment paper, flouring your hands and the dough as necessary. Top pizzas; bake for 12 to 15 minutes.

Yield: 2 pizza crusts

2 to 2½ cups (250 to 313 g) all-purpose einkorn flour, plus extra for sprinkling

2 tablespoons (30 ml) olive oil

2 teaspoons sea salt

1 packet (2¼ teaspoons [9 g]) active dry yeast

¼ cup (60 ml) plain kefir (or yogurt, but results vary)

¼ cup (60 ml) warm water (105 to 110°F [40 to 43°C])

STRAWBERRY LEEK PIZZA WITH KEFIR CRUST

The idea for combining strawberries and leeks came to us from Sara Forte's Sprouted Kitchen, where she put the two together in quesadillas. Here, the same winning combo tops our favorite thin and crispy einkorn pizza crust.

* Place crusts on parchment, brush with olive oil, and top with sautéed leeks, strawberries, mozzarella, salt, and pepper. Slide pizzas, one at a time, onto baking pan, and bake according to crust instructions. Serve with drizzles of balsamic vinegar and olive oil.

Yield: 2 pizzas

1 batch Thin and Crispy Pizza Crust (above), stretched into 2 pizzas

1 teaspoon (5 ml) olive oil, for brushing, plus more for finish

1 or 2 leeks, sliced, woody ends removed; sautéed in 1 tablespoon (13 g) coconut oil until soft

12 strawberries, chopped

16 ounces (453 g) fresh mozzarella

½ teaspoon each sea salt and black pepper

Balsamic vinegar, to finish

1. *On parchment, stretch and press the dough out with your fingers, pushing and flattening it into a large rectangle.*

3. *Top crust as you like, placing toppings almost to the edges.*

2. *When the dough is as thin as you can press it, add oil or sauce.*

4. *Bake pizzas at 475°F (250°C, or gas mark 9) for 12 to 15 minutes, then remove to cutting board to slice and serve.*

SOURDOUGH PIZZA CRUST

This pizza crust requires an overnight soak in the fridge, but besides that step, it's surprisingly simple. Compared with our thin and crispy crust (page 130), it's heartier, thicker, and more substantial, with that wonderful tang from sourdough. But we're basically obsessed with them both.

* A day beforehand, combine starter, warm water, olive oil, flour, and salt in a large bowl. Turn mixture onto floured surface and knead 5 to 7 minutes, until smooth. Form into ball, and place in an oiled bowl, turning to coat. Cover bowl with plastic. Refrigerate overnight. In the morning, remove bowl to counter and let sit at room temperature 4 to 5 hours.

* Place floured piece of parchment on counter and place dough on top. It will feel soft, elastic, and stretchy. With floured fingers, spread pizza out into a 14-inch (35 cm) square or a 15 x 13-inch (38 x 33 cm) rectangle. Cover with plastic wrap directly on parchment (to prevent skin), and let rest 2 hours.

* Preheat oven to 500°F (260°C, or gas mark 10) and place a pizza stone inside, if using. If you're not using a pizza stone, set the parchment and pizza on a large baking sheet, still with plastic covering it.

* Remove plastic from crust, add toppings, and bake 15 to 20 minutes, until golden. Move pizza to cutting board, brush edges with olive oil, and slice. Serve immediately. Leftover pizza may be refrigerated and reheated to serve.

Yield: 1 large pizza (8 to 12 large slices), or 2 medium (9-inch [23 cm]) pizzas

1 cup (250 g) unfed sourdough starter (straight from the fridge)

⅓ cup (78 ml) warm (105 to 110°F [40 to 43°c]) water

1 tablespoon (15 ml) olive oil

2¾ cups (344 g) all-purpose einkorn flour, plus more for dusting

1 teaspoon sea salt

PARSLEY PESTO PIZZA

*B*right, cheesy, and nutty, parsley pesto could make any pizza something special—but it pairs particularly well with the thick sourdough einkorn crust here.

✳ In a food processor, combine pesto ingredients and blend until smooth. Top sourdough pizza crust(s) with pesto, tomatoes, and mozzarella, and bake according to crust instructions.

Yield: 8 to 12 servings

FOR THE PARSLEY ALMOND PESTO:

2 cups (70 g) packed fresh parsley

½ cup (65 g) blanched almonds

2 cloves garlic

½ cup (50 g) Pecorino cheese

½ cup (120 ml) olive oil

1½ tablespoons (21 ml) fresh-squeezed lemon juice

FOR THE PIZZA:

1 Sourdough pizza crust (page 132)

4 Roma tomatoes, sliced into ¼-inch (6 mm) rounds

8 ounces (226 g) mozzarella

Recipe Note

• *If you have leftover pesto, thin it out with olive oil for a great salad dressing!*

STUFFED TOMATOES

This recipe uses a slight variation of the herbed tomato einkorn berry salad on page 91. Instead of chopping the tomatoes as you would for the salad, for this recipe, you hollow out the tomatoes and stuff the salad back inside, topping it with ricotta, bread crumbs, and olive oil, and then baking it for 30 minutes. What results is a savory, saucy mixture with Italian roots.

* Using a paring knife, cut a small circle around the stem of each tomato, removing it and throwing it away. Then, using a small spoon, scoop out all the tomato's fleshy insides and place them in a strainer set over a bowl, to let the juices drain. Set the tomato cavities in an 8 x 8-inch (20 x 20 cm) baking dish and salt all over (about 1 teaspoon total). Preheat oven to 350°F (180°C, or gas mark 4).

* In a large skillet, warm a tablespoon (15 ml) of olive oil and add half an onion, chopped. Sauté until translucent, adding the remaining salt and the pepper along the way. Add cooked, drained einkorn berries to the pan and stir. Add drained tomato flesh to the pan (discard juice or set aside for other use) and stir again. Add fresh herbs, stir, and add salt and pepper to taste. Spoon this filling into the prepared tomato cavities, filling all the way. Place a dollop of ricotta cheese on top of each tomato, then sprinkle bread crumbs all over everything. Bake, uncovered, for 30 to 40 minutes, until tomatoes are soft. Serve warm.

Yield: 10 stuffed tomatoes, or enough for 3 to 4 servings

10 medium tomatoes

1½ teaspoon sea salt, divided

1 tablespoon (15 ml) of olive oil, plus more for drizzling on tomatoes before baking

½ cup (80 g) chopped white onion

2¼ cups (428 g) Cooked Einkorn Berries (page 15)

¼ teaspoon black pepper

20 leaves of fresh basil, chopped

5 sprigs of parsley, chopped

4 sprigs of thyme, chopped

¼ to ½ cup (65 to 125 g) ricotta cheese

2 to 3 tablespoons (14 to 21 g) Herbed Bread Crumbs (page 70)

CHAPTER 7

Desserts

We met over ice pops, got engaged alongside cookies, and celebrated our wedding in a big white tent with a home-made pumpkin cake. We've always shared a sweet tooth. And while we may be the couple that doesn't keep white sugar in the house, we still manage to try new cookie ideas every other week. We stock up on dark chocolate when it's on sale. We have a giant gelato maker in our guest bed-room. So it's no surprise that the desserts chapter of this book was the easiest one for us to write.

❖ Chocolate Pear Cake 136
❖ Chocolate Layer Cake with Chocolate Buttercream 138
❖ Cannoli Cupcakes 139
❖ Small-Batch Vanilla Cupcakes with Butterscotch Buttercream 140
❖ Maple Ginger Shortcakes 141
❖ Grandma's Oatmeal Chocolate Chip Cookies 143
❖ Fudgey Cookies 144

❖ Spiced Cut-Out Cookies 145
❖ Spicy Chocolate Sandwich Cookies 146
❖ Pistachio Cranberry Cookies ..149
❖ Classic Anise Biscotti 150
❖ King-Size Chocolate Chip Currant Cookies 152
❖ Rosewater Sorghum Shortbread Cookies with Chocolate Drizzle 154
❖ Grape and Thyme Galette 155

❖ Flaky All-Butter Pie Crust 156
❖ Hearty, Whole-Grain Pie Crust 157
❖ Apple Dumplings 159
❖ Rustic Apple Tartlets 160
❖ Chocolate Blueberry Pie 161
❖ Fruit and Jam Tart on Maple Shortbread Cookie Crust 163
❖ Small-Batch Mini Cherry Banana Galettes 164
❖ Waffle Bowls 166

CHOCOLATE PEAR CAKE

A brownie-like cake gets taken up a notch in this recipe, as poached pears are placed directly in the batter while it bakes. Beyond the obvious appeal of chocolate paired with fruit, this cake is visually stunning, especially when sliced.

* Preheat oven to 350°F (180°C, or gas mark 4). Grease a 9 x 5-inch (23 x 13 cm) loaf pan, and line it with parchment paper so that some hangs over each long side (this will make it easy to remove cake after baking).

* Place a saucepan over medium heat and fill it with enough water to be 3 inches (7.5 cm) deep. Add vanilla bean and coconut sugar, and bring to a boil. Add pears and simmer this mixture for 12 to 15 minutes, until pears are fork tender. Remove pears to separate plate with a slotted spoon.

* Meanwhile, while pears are cooking, melt butter in a saucepan over medium heat and remove immediately to cool.

* In a large bowl, combine flour, sugar, salt, baking soda, and cocoa powder. Add cooled butter and water, and stir together mixture until well combined. Spoon this thick mixture into the prepared loaf pan, spreading it evenly in the pan, where it will fill about half-way to the top (it rises generously while baking). Place the poached pears into the cake batter, spacing them apart evenly and standing them upright.

* Bake cake for 40 to 50 minutes, until a toothpick inserted in the center comes out clean. Let cool in pan for 10 minutes before lifting cake with parchment out of pan. Set on a wire rack to continue cooling. Serve sliced, warm or at room temperature.

Yield: One 9 x 5-inch (23 x 13 cm) loaf, or 12 to 18 servings

FOR THE POACHED PEARS:

1 vanilla bean

½ cup (80 g) coconut sugar

2 bosc pears, peeled and bottom cores removed

FOR THE CAKE:

6 tablespoons (85 g) butter

1½ cups (188 g) all-purpose einkorn flour

1 cup (160 g) coconut sugar

½ teaspoon sea salt

1 teaspoon baking soda

⅓ cup (30 g) cocoa powder

¾ cup (175 ml) water

CHOCOLATE LAYER CAKE WITH CHOCOLATE BUTTERCREAM

Even for a dessert made with all natural ingredients, this cake is definitely decadent. We think of it as a celebration cake—the perfect thing for a big birthday party or family gathering where everybody gets one moist, rich, memorable slice. Also, if three layers sounds too rich, cut everything by three, and bake the mixture in one pan.

* Preheat oven to 350°F (180°C, or gas mark 4) and grease three 9-inch (23 cm) round (or see recipe note) cake pans.

* In a large bowl, stir together flour, sugar, cocoa powder, baking soda, baking powder, and salt. Use a hand mixer or stand mixer to blend in coconut oil, butter, yogurt, eggs, and vanilla extract. The batter will be thick and sticky. Once it's fully blended, pour in the hot water, stirring gently with a spoon to prevent splattering. The mixture will be thin and runny at this point, thinner than a typical cake batter.

* Pour the mixture into the prepared pans. Bake for 30 to 35 minutes, or until a toothpick inserted in the centers comes out clean. Cool completely on wire racks before removing from pans.

* For frosting: In a large bowl, use a hand mixer to blend softened butter and powdered coconut sugar until creamy and soft. Add cocoa powder and heavy cream, and blend until the mixture reaches a buttercream consistency—thick and spreadable—about 5 minutes.

* Top the cake layers with blackberry jam and frost the entire exterior of the cake with buttercream. The cake is best served at room temperature.

Yield: 10 to 12 servings

FOR THE CAKE:

3 cups (375 g) all-purpose einkorn flour

1¾ cups (280 g) coconut sugar

¾ cup (45 g) cocoa powder

1 tablespoon (15 g) baking soda

1 tablespoon (15 g) baking powder

1½ teaspoons sea salt

1½ cups (356 ml) coconut oil, melted (or olive oil)

¾ cup (168 g) unsalted butter, melted

1½ cups (345 g) full-fat yogurt

3 eggs

1 tablespoon (15 ml) vanilla extract

1½ cups (356 ml) hot water

FOR THE BUTTERCREAM:

1½ cups (336 g) butter, room temperature

1½ cups (240 g) coconut sugar, powdered in Vitamix or food processor

¾ cup (65 g) cocoa powder

1 cup (240 ml) heavy cream

FOR THE FILLING:

10 ounces (280 g) blackberry jam (or other fruit jam)

CANNOLI CUPCAKES

Take the filling inside a cannoli shell and stuff it inside and on top of yellow cupcakes. You get a throwback to Italian bakeries and a real showstopper in terms of visual appeal.

The cupcakes themselves may be baked ahead of time and frozen, so long as they're thawed a day before frosting/serving. It's best to frost them the day you want to serve them, but the ricotta filling must be strained overnight, so prepare that the day before hand.

* Preheat the oven to 350°F (180°C, or gas mark 4). Grease or line two 12-cup muffin pans.

* In a large bowl, use a hand mixer or stand mixer to cream together the powdered sugar with softened butter and olive oil. Beat in 4 eggs, one at a time, and add vanilla. In a separate, medium bowl, sift flour, baking powder, and salt. In a small bowl, whisk together milk, yogurt, and water. To the large bowl of butter-sugar mixture, add flour mixture and milk mixture alternately, mixing after each addition. Once everything is combined, divide batter evenly among muffin cups.

* Bake cupcakes 25 to 35 minutes, until a toothpick inserted in the center comes out clean. Remove from pan to another surface as soon as you can to prevent the cakes from falling (although if they do, don't panic: the frosting will hide it). Let cool completely.

* Line a strainer with cheesecloth, place ricotta in the strainer over a bowl, and cover with plastic wrap and a towel. Weigh it down with a heavy object, and let drain in the refrigerator overnight.

* In a large bowl, using a hand mixer or stand mixer, beat ricotta until smooth and creamy. Add sugar, cinnamon, and vanilla, and blend until smooth. Stir in zest. Fold in the chopped chocolate and refrigerate for up to 24 hours, or use right away.

* Cutting a cone shape out of the top of each cupcake (eat or save these scraps for later). Then, stuff the holes with ricotta filling, and spread on top. Sprinkle on chopped pistachios for garnish and serve.

Yield: 20 to 24 cupcakes

FOR THE CUPCAKES:

1½ cups (240 g) coconut sugar or Sucanat, powdered in a Vitamix or food processor

½ cup (225 g) unsalted butter, softened

½ cup (120 ml) olive oil

4 eggs

2 teaspoons vanilla extract

2¾ cups (344 g) all-purpose einkorn flour

1 tablespoon (14 g) baking powder

1 teaspoon sea salt

1¼ cup (295 ml) whole milk

½ cup (115 g) full-fat yogurt

¼ cup (60 ml) water

FOR THE FILLING/TOPPING:

32 ounces (1 kg) whole-milk ricotta cheese

1½ cups (240 g) coconut sugar or Sucanat, sifted and ground in a Vitamix or food processor

½ teaspoon cinnamon

1 teaspoon vanilla extract

1¾ ounces (50 g) dark chocolate, chopped finely

Zest of 1 lemon

Chopped pistachios, for topping

SMALL-BATCH VANILLA CUPCAKES WITH BUTTERSCOTCH BUTTERCREAM

When you want a small batch of sweet treats, this 8-cupcake version is just the ticket. From its light, moist cake to its rich butterscotch frosting, this recipe yields a decadent dessert that feels both indulgent and satisfying.

Don't swap the coconut sugar in the frosting! If you swap in plain organic powdered sugar for the powdered coconut sugar, you will lose the butterscotch flavor and wind up with overpowering sweetness.

* Preheat oven to 350°F (180°C or gas mark 4) and line 8 muffin cups with liners.

* In a large bowl, use a stand mixer or hand mixer to cream together butter and sugar. Add eggs and vanilla, and continue to combine. Add flour, baking, powder, baking soda, and salt, and combine. At this point, the batter should look like frosting; add yogurt, and mix until incorporated.

* Divide batter among 8 prepared muffin cups. If using a 12-cup muffin pan, fill empty muffin holders halfway with water. Bake cupcakes for 20 to 30 minutes, until a toothpick inserted in the center comes out clean. Let cool before frosting.

* To make the frosting, use a stand mixer or hand mixer to blend butter, powdered coconut sugar, milk, flour, and vanilla extract in a large bowl, until smooth and whipped. Frost cupcakes and serve immediately. Leftover cupcakes should be stored in the refrigerator and will last up to a week.

Recipe Note

• *Flour in the frosting? We know it seems unusual, but ever since our friend Christina told us about adding a little flour to buttercream, we've loved pairing this version with cupcakes. Prepare yourself for a rich, creamy frosting that could work with any of your favorite cakes.*

Yield: 8 cupcakes

FOR THE CUPCAKES:

6 tablespoons (60 g) butter, softened

6 tablespoons (60 g) coconut sugar

2 eggs

1 tablespoon (15 ml) vanilla extract

1¼ cup (125 g) freshly ground, sifted einkorn flour

½ teaspoon baking powder

½ teaspoon baking soda

½ teaspoon sea salt

2 tablespoons (30 g) yogurt

FOR THE FROSTING:

¼ cup (55 g) butter, softened

1 cup (160 g) coconut sugar, powdered in food processor or Vitamix

2 tablespoons (30 ml) milk

1 tablespoon (16 g) all-purpose einkorn flour

1 teaspoon vanilla extract

MAPLE GINGER SHORTCAKES

Try a new spin on shortcakes with this recipe, which dresses up the traditional shortcake with maple syrup and ginger. On their own, these shortcakes are sugar-kissed biscuits, firm and sweet and dry; paired with ice cream and fruit, they're a delicious dessert hard to resist.

* Preheat oven to 375°F (190°C, or gas mark 5) and line a baking sheet with parchment paper. In a large bowl, use a big spoon to stir together the first five ingredients. Cut in butter with a pastry cutter or 2 forks, until butter is broken up into chunks throughout, about 15 to 20 seconds. Stir in yogurt and egg until well combined. Use clean, floured hands to press and shape mixture into a ball of dough.

* On a floured surface and with a floured rolling pin, roll dough out into a 7-inch (18 cm) circle that's ½ inch (13 mm) thick. Cut out shortcakes using a 3-inch (7.5 cm) biscuit or cookie cutter. Gather together remaining dough, roll out to ½ inch (13 mm) thick and cut out shortcakes again until there's no more dough. If you wind up with a little extra dough beyond the 6 shortcakes, freeform it into a smaller shortcake.

* Place the shortcakes on a baking sheet, sprinkle the tops with raw sugar, and bake 13 to 16 minutes, until golden brown on top. Serve with whipped cream and fruit, ice cream, or whatever you like.

Yield: 6 or 7 shortcakes

1⅔ cups (208 g) all-purpose einkorn flour

3 tablespoons (60 g) maple syrup

2 teaspoons baking powder

2 teaspoons ginger powder

½ teaspoon sea salt

6 tablespoons (85 g) unsalted butter, cold and cubed into tablespoons (14 g)

3 tablespoons (45 g) yogurt

1 egg

1 tablespoon (13 g) raw sugar, for dusting

GRANDMA'S OATMEAL CHOCOLATE CHIP COOKIES

There is no cookie I've been making longer than my grandma's crisp oatmeal chocolate chip cookies. In this einkorn version of her classic, we use butter and coconut oil instead of her called-for margarine, slightly different ingredient proportions, dark chocolate instead of chocolate chips, and unrefined sugar instead of both white and brown—but the crunchy, flavorful treats that emerge from the oven are every bit the way I remember them.

✳ Preheat oven to 325°F (160°C, or gas mark 3) and line 2 baking sheets with parchment paper. In a large bowl, use a wooden spoon to stir together all ingredients except the oats and chocolate, until well mixed. Add the oats and chopped chocolate and stir until just combined.

✳ Drop dough by the spoonful onto prepared baking sheets, leaving at least an inch (2.5 cm) between cookies. Bake for 12 to 15 minutes, rotating sheets halfway through, until firm and golden.

Yield: 20 cookies

¼ cup (57 g) butter, softened

¼ cup (57 g) coconut oil, softened

1 cup (160 g) Sucanat

1 egg

1 teaspoon vanilla

1 cup (125 g) all-purpose einkorn flour

½ teaspoon baking soda

1 teaspoon baking powder

½ teaspoon sea salt

1½ cups (150 g) old-fashioned oats

3½ ounces (100 g) dark chocolate, chopped

FUDGEY COOKIES

These nutty chocolate treats pair finely ground pecans with a cocoa-flavored cookie batter studded with chocolate chunks throughout. A must for the chocolate lover, these fudgey cookies are just begging for a tall glass of milk.

* Preheat oven to 350°F (180°C, or gas mark 4). Grind pecan pieces in a food processor until as fine as pecan meal.

* In a large bowl, combine einkorn flour, cocoa powder, baking powder, baking soda, coconut sugar, and salt. In a separate bowl, combine maple syrup, molasses, vanilla, and coconut oil. Stir wet ingredients into the dry ingredients; add ground pecans and chopped chocolate and stir together well.

* Put the bowl of batter in the fridge for 10 minutes and line 2 baking sheets with parchment paper. Spoon balls of dough onto prepared baking sheets and sprinkle a little salt on top. Bake for 10 to 15 minutes, until firm and set.

Yield: 20 cookies

½ cup (55 g) pecan pieces

1¼ cups (156 g) all-purpose einkorn flour

¼ cup (31 g) cocoa powder

1 teaspoon baking powder

1 teaspoon baking soda

¼ cup (25 g) coconut sugar

½ teaspoon sea salt, plus extra for sprinkling on top

½ cup (160 g) maple syrup

½ teaspoon molasses

1½ teaspoon vanilla extract

½ cup (120 ml) melted coconut oil

3½ ounces (100 g) dark chocolate, chopped into small pieces

SPICED CUT-OUT COOKIES

I hate to admit it, but I've never loved gingerbread—but these soft, spiced cut-out cookies are another story. Dark and fragrant, they carry a punch of ginger with cinnamon, nutmeg, and cardamom.

* In a large bowl, cream together butter and sugar with a hand mixer. Add egg, molasses, and extracts, and mix until just combined.

* In a separate bowl, combine all of the remaining ingredients. Add this mixture to the butter-sugar mixture and combine until dough forms a ball.

* Wrap dough in plastic and chill for an hour or up to overnight in the fridge; or freeze for up to a month, thawing overnight in the fridge when you're ready to use.

* When ready to make cookies, remove dough from fridge and let rest on counter for at least 10 minutes before separating it into 2 equal pieces. Meanwhile, preheat oven to 400°F (200°C, or gas mark 6) and line 2 baking sheets with parchment paper.

* Working with one half at a time, roll the dough out on a floured surface to approximately ⅛ inch (3 mm) thick. Cut out cookies as you like, placing them on parchment sheets.

* Bake cookies for 8 to 10 minutes, rotating sheets halfway through, until centers appear just baked through.

Yield: 24 medium-size cookies

½ cup (112 g) unsalted butter, softened

½ cup (80 g) Sucanat or coconut sugar

1 egg

1 tablespoon (20 g) molasses

½ teaspoon vanilla extract

¼ teaspoon almond extract

1⅔ cups (208 g) all-purpose einkorn flour, plus more for dusting

2 teaspoons baking soda

½ teaspoon sea salt

1 tablespoon (6 g) ground ginger

2 teaspoons ground cinnamon

1 teaspoon ground nutmeg

1 teaspoon cardamom powder

SPICY CHOCOLATE SANDWICH COOKIES

*W*e got engaged on a spring day in Nashville, sitting on a blue blanket in a quiet park, alongside a basket filled with a full picnic spread that included a version of these cookies. In this einkorn version of that memory, we pair the firm chocolate cookies with a sweet buttercream that counters the kick of the cayenne.

* In a medium-size bowl, combine flour, cocoa powder, baking soda, salt, cinnamon, ginger, black pepper, and cayenne. In a large bowl, cream sugar, butter, and coconut oil together with a hand mixer. Add vanilla, followed by dry ingredients. Beat on low speed until fully incorporated. Finally, add egg; the batter will transform from what looks like crumbly dirt to what's closer to clay-like mud.

* Form dough into a solid log about 6 inches (15 cm) long and 2½ inches (6 cm) in diameter. Wrap in waxed paper or parchment. Chill for at least 45 minutes.

* Preheat oven to 350°F (180°C, or gas mark 4) and line 2 baking sheets with parchment paper. Take out the log of dough and use a sharp knife to slice rounds just under ¼ inch (6 mm) thick. Place the rounds an inch (2.5 cm) or so apart on prepared baking sheets and bake 12 to 14 minutes, until cookies puff and crackle on top and begin to settle slightly. Let the cookies cool completely before frosting; any cookies that won't be eaten immediately may be stored, unfilled, in an airtight container for up to 2 weeks (or frozen for up to 2 months).

* Just before serving, beat butter, powdered Sucanat or sugar, and vanilla in a large bowl with a hand mixer or stand mixer until smooth. Spread a spoonful of this mixture on the underside of half of the cooled cookies, and top each with a remaining cookie.

Yield: 12 cookie sandwiches

FOR THE COOKIES:

1¼ cups (156 g) all-purpose einkorn flour

½ cup (43 g) cocoa powder

¼ teaspoon baking soda

¼ teaspoon sea salt

¾ teaspoon ground cinnamon

¼ teaspoon ginger powder

⅛ teaspoon black pepper

⅛ teaspoon cayenne pepper

1 cup (160 g) Sucanat (unrefined cane sugar)

5 tablespoons (69 g) unsalted butter, room temperature

2 tablespoons (26 g) coconut oil, softened

½ teaspoon vanilla extract

1 egg

FOR THE FILLING:

½ cup (112 g) butter, room temperature

1 cup (160 g) Sucanat, powdered in a food processor (or powdered sugar)

1 teaspoon vanilla extract

PISTACHIO CRANBERRY COOKIES

*I*f you like oatmeal raisin cookies, you'll love these little cranberry cookies, which mimic the texture, but add the unmistakable twist of pistachios and tang of cranberries into the mix—and, like oatmeal raisin cookies, they may have a soft, chewy texture if you take them early in the bake time, or they may achieve a crisp, firm texture if you let them go longer.

✳ Preheat oven to 350°F (180°C, or gas mark 4) and line 2 baking sheets with parchment paper.

✳ Grind pistachios in a food processor until they crumble, about 20 to 30 seconds; they should not quite be the texture of pistachio meal or flour, but rather like a coarse, pebbly mixture of tiny nut pieces.

✳ In a medium bowl, stir together pistachios with einkorn flour, baking powder, baking soda, and Sucanat. In a separate, larger bowl, whisk together olive oil, molasses, vanilla extract, and egg. Add the dry mixture to the wet one, stirring until combined. Stir in cranberries.

✳ Scoop dough into 1-inch (2.5 cm) balls, and place on prepared baking sheets. The cookies won't spread while baking, so you may fit as many as 10 to 12 to a sheet. Bake 12 to 15 minutes, until golden around the edges and just slightly moist in the centers; bake less for softer cookies, longer for firmer ones.

✳ Immediately after removing baking sheets, slide the parchment onto another surface and flatten each cookie with a spatula. Let cool slightly before eating. Leftover cookies may be stored in an airtight container for about a week or frozen for several months.

Yield: 24 cookies

1 cup (135 g) dry-roasted, salted pistachio meats

1 cup (125 g) all-purpose einkorn flour

1 teaspoon baking powder

½ teaspoon baking soda

¾ cup (120 g) Sucanat

½ cup (120 ml) olive oil

½ teaspoon molasses

2 teaspoons vanilla extract

1 egg

⅔ cup (100 g) dried, sweetened cranberries

CLASSIC ANISE BISCOTTI

When we bring a tin of cookies to our families' houses at Christmastime, these classic anise biscotti are the first to go. Crisp and crunchy, they're perfect for dunking in hot tea or coffee, and they're also nice with milk. We like to melt chocolate and drizzle it over the cookies as a finishing, sweetening touch, but with or without the icing, they're one of our all-time favorites.

✳ Preheat oven to 350°F (180°C, or gas mark 4). Line a baking sheet with parchment paper. In a large mixing bowl, cream together coconut sugar and softened butter until they come together. Add eggs one at a time, beating after each addition; blend in almond extract. In a separate bowl, combine flour, baking powder, sea salt, nutmeg, and anise seed.

✳ Slowly add in dry ingredients to wet, until the dough is a thick, heavy, and sticky mixture. Turn the dough out in one big mound onto the parchment-lined baking sheet, and with wet hands form a long rectangular log. You can form the log to your own preference, if you like. We shoot for a rectangle that is 12½ x 4½ inches (32 x 12 cm) and 1 inch (2.5 cm) thick. Once formed, bake dough for 30 to 35 minutes, until slightly brown around the edges and firm to the touch (the inside will still be moist). Remove from oven and cool completely.

✳ Reduce oven temperature to 225°F (107°C, or gas mark ½). Cut the cooled log diagonally into long, 1-inch (2.5 cm)-thick slices. Carefully place the slices on a baking sheet and bake for 75 to 90 minutes, flipping halfway through. Remove and let cool. Serve plain or drizzled with chocolate, as instructed below.

✳ For the optional chocolate glaze: Melt chocolate in a double boiler by heating water in a saucepan and setting a bowl on top with the chocolate in it, stirring while it heats. Once it's melted, drizzle the chocolate over the cooled biscotti. Let glaze cool completely before storing the biscotti in an airtight container.

Yield: 16 to 18 biscotti

1½ cups (240 g) coconut sugar

¾ cup (167 g) butter, softened

2 eggs

2 teaspoons almond extract

3 cups (375 g) all-purpose einkorn flour

2 teaspoons baking powder

1 teaspoon sea salt

⅛ teaspoon nutmeg

3 tablespoons (24 g) anise seed

3½ ounces (100 g) dark chocolate, chopped (optional)

KING-SIZE CHOCOLATE CHIP CURRANT COOKIES

Yield: 8 king-size cookies

6 tablespoons (85 g) unsalted butter, cold and cubed into half tablespoons (7 g)

1 cup (160 g) coconut sugar

1 tablespoon (15 ml) whole milk

2 teaspoons pure vanilla extract

1 egg yolk

1¼ cups (156 g) all-purpose einkorn flour

1 teaspoon baking powder

½ teaspoon baking soda

½ teaspoon sea salt

½ cup (113 g) currants

2 ounces (57 g) chopped chocolate

*W*e must have tested a dozen different versions of einkorn chocolate chip cookies before arriving at this one, which is loosely adapted from a method in Kim Boyce's *Good to the Grain*. Rather than softening the butter or melting and cooling it before creaming, this technique calls for cold, cubed butter to be mixed with the sugar upfront. When you use a hand mixer, the process can be a little messy, but with a little patience and some elbow grease, the butter and sugar meld together well (if you find this too frustrating, you might want to use a food processor to mix the batter instead, which is what we typically do). What results are enormous, bakery-size cookies firm enough to hold with your fingers, cracked on top, and both crisp around the edges and soft and chewy inside.

As for add-ins, there's no reason not to get creative with this cookie base. While we used currants and chocolate, feel free to try your favorite chopped nut, dried fruit, or candy in their place.

* Preheat oven to 350°F (180°C, or gas mark 4) and line 2 baking sheets with parchment. In a large bowl, cream together butter and sugar with a hand mixer (it may be a little messy at first) or in a food processor until it's fully incorporated, creamy, and almost whipped. Add milk and vanilla and combine. Add egg yolk and combine.

* In a medium bowl, stir together dry ingredients. Add this mixture to the first bowl or food processor and mix. Stir in currants and chocolate chips.

* Use an ice cream scooper to spoon out large mounds of dough the size of tennis balls (roughly 2½ tablespoons, or 37 g each). Form these mounds into balls with your hands and place them on the parchment-lined sheets, 4 to a sheet, with plenty of space between them. Bake 15 to 20 minutes, rotating the pans halfway through, until cracked and set.

ROSEWATER SORGHUM SHORTBREAD COOKIES WITH CHOCOLATE DRIZZLE

*S*weetened only with sorghum syrup, these rosewater short-bread cookies are truly unique. Each bite provides a light floral note amid the sort of tea-cookie texture we remember from the packaged cookies of our childhood. If you can't find sorghum syrup, swap in maple syrup—the taste will be slightly altered, but the light, dry texture, perfect for pairing with tea, will remain.

✳ Preheat oven to 350°F (180°C, or gas mark 4) and line 2 baking sheets with parchment paper.

✳ In a large bowl, mix flour, cornstarch, and sea salt. Cut in butter with a pastry cutter or 2 forks, until you get small pea-size pieces throughout. Add sorghum syrup, egg yolks, and rosewater. Mix with a fork and form a ball of dough.

✳ Gently press or roll the dough on a floured surface to between ¼ inch and ½ inch (6 and 13 mm). Using a cookie or biscuit cutter, cut out cookies and bake on prepared baking sheets for 12 to 15 minutes, until edges are golden.

✳ Once cookies have cooled, make the chocolate drizzle by melting chocolate and sorghum syrup in a double boiler and drizzling across the tops of the cookies as you like. Serve with hot drinks if desired.

Yield: 30 small or 15 large cookies

FOR THE COOKIES:

2 cups (250 g) all-purpose einkorn flour

3 tablespoons (45 g) non-GMO cornstarch

¼ teaspoon sea salt

10 tablespoons (145 g) chilled butter, cubed into tablespoons

5 tablespoons (100 g) sorghum syrup

3 large egg yolks

1 tablespoon (15 ml) rosewater

FOR THE CHOCOLATE DRIZZLE:

2 ounces (57 g) dark chocolate

1 to 2 teaspoons sorghum syrup (to taste, depending on how dark your chocolate is)

GRAPE AND THYME GALETTE

To us, a grape galette is summer picnic food, the sort of thing easy to package up and eat with your hands on a blanket in the grass. That doesn't mean it isn't refined and elegant, however: pairing grapes with thyme in the filling here creates a sophisticated, complex flavor that's both sweet and herbal.

Because of the liquidic nature of the grape filling, we bake this galette on parchment inside a rimmed baking dish, such as a tart pan or rimmed baking sheet.

* Line a rimmed baking pan or tart pan with parchment paper (see headnote). In a medium bowl, combine flour and salt. Cut in the cubed butter with a pastry cutter or forks or, potentially, inside a food processor. Add water and yogurt; stir until it comes together and use your hands to form the dough into a ball. Roll out on a floured surface to be larger than you'd like your galette to be. Place on a prepared baking sheet or pan. While you make the filling, stick this dough in the fridge to keep it cold.

* Preheat oven to 350°F (180°C, or gas mark 4). To make the filling, combine grapes, coconut sugar, arrowroot powder, thyme, and lime juice in a bowl; stir to coat.

* Remove the chilled galette dough from the fridge. Pile the filling in the center and fold the edges on top of the grapes, pleating it as you do. The idea is just to get the edges folded up and over the filling to keep them securely inside while they bake.

* Brush the dough with yogurt to give the galette a beautifully golden crust as it bakes. Place the galette in the oven for 45 minutes to a little over an hour, rotating once halfway through. The galette is done when the crust is golden and firm. Let cool before slicing.

Yield: 1 rustic grape galette, around 6 to 8 servings

FOR THE CRUST:

1¼ cups (156 g) all-purpose einkorn flour

½ teaspoon sea salt

½ cup (112 g) butter, cold and cubed into half tablespoons (7 g)

¼ cup (60 ml) cold water

1 tablespoon (15 g) plain (nonflavored) yogurt

FOR THE FILLING:

2½ cups (500 g) quartered grapes

2 tablespoons (26 g) coconut palm sugar

2 tablespoons (16 g) arrowroot powder

5 to 6 sprigs of thyme (pull off the leaves)

2 tablespoons (30 ml) lime juice

FOR BRUSHING THE DOUGH:

2 to 3 tablespoons (15 to 30 g) of yogurt

FLAKY ALL-BUTTER PIE CRUST

I inherited a version of this perfect pie crust from my mom and my grandma, and it does come with a learning curve. The way you work the butter into the mixture is different from most recipes. The cold butter is in chunks rather than pebbles, and it only comes together when you quickly (in seconds!) work the dough with your hands. The benefit is no chill time (though you may chill it for later use if you like; simply thaw before using).

* Combine flour and salt in a medium bowl. Using a pastry cutter, cut in the cubed butter until the butter is in random chunks throughout, larger than peas but smaller than dimes. The chunks don't need to be identical, and there can still be some big ones throughout, but you're aiming to get all the (still cold) butter broken up—this should only take about 15 to 20 seconds.

* Stir in water; the mixture will still look crumbly, and you'll think you need to add more water, but resist the impulse. Instead, use floured hands to push, press, and form the crumbly mixture into a soft, workable ball. This entire process should take no more than 3 to 5 minutes. If it's too dry to work with, add another tablespoon (15 ml) of water; if it's too wet, add another tablespoon (8 g) of flour; repeat until dough will come together into a ball.

* Set dough on a well-floured surface. Using a floured rolling pin, roll the dough with quick, swift strokes. Gently flip and continue rolling, turning it every few strokes to reflour the surface and keep it from sticking to the counter. Note that you will see streaks of butter throughout the dough—this is good; it's what will impart the flaky texture once it bakes. Those streaks of butter may also make the dough sticky, however, so don't be afraid to dust it with flour generously as you work.

* Roll dough into a circle a little larger than your pie plate. Gently transfer the dough to your pie plate and form to fit, pressing around the sides with your fingers to make a design if you like. Prebake or fill and bake according to pie recipe instructions.

Yield: 1 pie crust

1 cup (125 g) all-purpose einkorn flour, plus more for surfaces

½ teaspoon sea salt

½ cup (112 g) unsalted butter, cold and cubed into 16 pieces

¼ cup (60 ml) cold water

Recipe Note

• *Using all butter—and such a high proportion of it—is what gives this pie crust its addictive, flaky quality.*

HEARTY WHOLE-GRAIN PIE CRUST

This whole-grain version of our flaky pie crust requires more flour and less liquid than its all-purpose flour counterpart, but it emerges from the oven just as beautifully golden and firm. As with our other pie crust, this recipe requires no chilling. Instead, the same effect that is derived from chilled dough—cold butter that melts in the crust as it bakes, forming air pockets and flakiness—occurs in a quicker process. Dough may also be chilled for later use if you like; simply let thaw before using.

* Combine flour and salt in a medium bowl. Using a pastry cutter, cut in the cubed butter until the butter is in random chunks throughout, larger than peas but smaller than dimes. The chunks don't need to be identical, and there can still be some big ones, but you're aiming to get all the (still cold) butter broken up—this should only take about 15 to 20 seconds.

* Stir in water; the mixture will still look crumbly, and you'll think you need to add more water, but resist the impulse. Instead, use your floured hands to push, press, and form the crumbly mixture into a soft, workable ball. This entire process should take no more than 3 to 5 minutes. If it's too dry to work with, add another tablespoon (15 ml) of water; if it's too wet, add another tablespoon (7 g) of flour; repeat until dough will come together into a ball.

* Set dough on a well-floured surface. Using a floured rolling pin, roll the dough with quick, swift strokes. Gently flip and continue rolling, turning it every few strokes to reflour the surface and keep it from sticking to the counter. Note that you will see streaks of butter throughout the dough—this is good; it's what will impart the flaky texture once it bakes. Those streaks of butter may also make the dough sticky however, so don't be afraid to dust it with flour generously as you work.

* Roll dough into a circle that is a little larger than your pie plate. Gently transfer the dough to your pie plate and form to fit, pressing around the sides with your fingers to make a design if you like. Prebake or fill and bake according to pie recipe instructions.

Yield: 1 pie crust

1¼ cups (125 g) sifted (to remove bran) whole-grain einkorn flour, plus more for surfaces

½ teaspoon sea salt

7 tablespoons unsalted butter (100 g), cold and cubed into 14 pieces

1 to 2 tablespoons (15 to 30 ml) cold water

APPLE DUMPLINGS

*D*umplings are such a brilliant invention: Fill fruit with sugar, spices, and nuts; wrap it in pastry dough; and bake until the fruit is soft and the dough crisp and golden. They're like individual apple pies, but simpler! When we eat these warm dumplings, topped with ice cream, we give thanks to whomever first came up with this creation—as comforting as it is decadent.

* Begin by combining einkorn flour, salt, and Sucanat in a large bowl. Use a pastry cutter or 2 forks to cut the cubed butter into the mixture until the butter is broken up into chunks throughout. Stir in up to ½ cup (120 ml) water, mixing until the water is absorbed and the crumbs start to come together. Then, using clean hands, press and push the mixture into a large, smooth ball of dough. Separate this ball of dough into 5 equal portions, form them into balls, and wrap them in plastic wrap. Place in the fridge to chill while you make the dumpling filling.

* Preheat oven to 375°F (190°C, or gas mark 5) and grease a baking pan large enough to hold all 5 apples snugly. Peel and core apples. In a small bowl, combine Sucanat, cinnamon, currants, and pecans.

* Remove 1 ball of dough at a time to a floured surface, rolling it out into a piece large enough to wrap up and around an apple. Place a cored apple in the center, and fill the middle alternately with the Sucanat mixture and pieces of butter. Lift the dough up and over the apple, pressing to create a firm sleeve around the entire fruit. Set the dough-wrapped apple in the baking dish. Repeat with remaining dough and apples until all are snugly in the baking dish.

* Brush the dough around the apples with yogurt and bake for 45 minutes to an hour, until golden. Serve with ice cream, if desired.

Yield: 5 dumplings

FOR THE PASTRY DOUGH:

2 cups (250 g) all-purpose einkorn flour

1 teaspoon sea salt

1 tablespoon (13 g) Sucanat

¾ cup (167 g) butter, cold and cubed into 24 pieces

½ cup (120 ml) cold water

5 apples

FOR THE DUMPLING FILLING:

2½ tablespoons (33 g) Sucanat

½ tablespoon (3 g) cinnamon

1 tablespoon (8 g) currants

1 tablespoon (14 g) crushed pecans

3 tablespoons (42 g) butter, diced

2 tablespoons (30 g) yogurt

RUSTIC APPLE TARTLETS

While these tartlets are simple, they are also pretty as a picture and sized perfectly for sweet appetizers, if not desserts. They are made, essentially, by cutting little rounds of pie crust and topping with sweetened apples, fresh thyme, and toasted hazelnuts before baking in the oven. We dare you to eat just one.

* Start by making the pastry crust: In a large bowl, combine flour and salt. Cut butter into this mixture with a pastry cutter or 2 forks, until there are no more big chunks of butter and the mixture looks like coarse crumbs Add water, stir until it's mixed, and then use your hands to work the dough into a solid dough, adding more flour if needed. Form dough into a ball and set in a bowl in the fridge.

* Preheat oven to 350°F (180°C, or gas mark 4). In a medium-size bowl, mix apples, lemon juice, cinnamon, and honey.

* Roll pastry dough out on parchment paper or a floured surface to be ½ inch (13 mm) thick, and cut out twelve 3-inch (7.6 cm) rounds, using a cookie or biscuit cutter.

* Arrange apple slices on top of the rounds, adding a little drizzle of honey and some thyme to each one. Bake for 30 to 45 minutes, until apples turn slightly golden. Garnish with more honey and chopped hazelnuts.

Yield: 12 tartlets

FOR THE PASTRY DOUGH:

1 to 1⅓ cup (125 to 166 g) all-purpose‚ einkorn flour

½ teaspoon sea salt

½ cup (112 g) cold, cubed unsalted butter

¼ cup (60 ml) cold water

FOR THE TOPPING:

3 apples, peeled and sliced as uniformly as possible

2 tablespoons (30 ml) fresh-squeezed lemon juice

2 teaspoons cinnamon

1 to 2 teaspoons honey, plus more for drizzling

Fresh thyme, to taste

½ cup (58 g) toasted hazelnuts, chopped

CHOCOLATE BLUEBERRY PIE

It seems to us that the combination of blueberry and chocolate does not get enough attention. We always hear about strawberries and chocolate or raspberries and chocolate, but let's be honest—chocolate goes with just about everything, especially when it comes to fruit. If you love strong, dark chocolate, then you will like this recipe. It is not overly sweet, and the dark chocolate melts in with the blueberry mixture.

Served warm, the pie is like a sophisticated, richer version of blueberry pie; served cold, it's like blueberry pie with chocolate chunks.

* Preheat oven to 350°F (180°C, or gas mark 4) and butter a 9-inch (23 cm) pie plate.

* Make the berry filling: Add 2 cups (290 g) of the blueberries to a bowl and add the coconut sugar, lemon juice, and arrowroot powder. Take a masher or large fork and mash the berries until some of the juices start to flow, and the mixture gets liquidy. All of the berries do not have to be mashed, just enough that the mixture starts to liquefy. Add the chopped chocolate and the remaining blueberries. Stir to coat the berries with the mixture.

* On a floured surface, roll out the first ball of pie dough until it is slightly larger than your pie plate. Lay in the plate, letting the extra overhang around the edges. Add the blueberry mixture to the pie plate. Roll out the second ball of dough to be slightly larger than the pie plate and lay it on top of the blueberry mixture in the pie pan. Use the excess dough around the edges to create a decorative crust, trimming off anything too big, folding over the extras, and pinching together the crusts and/or using a fork to press them together.

* Brush pie with yogurt or kefir, and bake 60 to 65 minutes, until the crust is golden. Serve warm or cold.

Yield: One 9-inch (23 cm) pie, or 6 to 8 servings

5½ cups (800 g) fresh blueberries, divided

½ cup (80 g) coconut sugar

1½ tablespoons (21 ml) lemon juice

3 tablespoons (21 g) arrowroot starch/powder

3.2 ounces (91 g) dark chocolate, chopped roughly (we used 85 percent dark)

2 batches Einkorn Pie Crust (page 156 or 157)

2 to 3 tablespoons (30 to 45 g) yogurt or kefir

FRUIT AND JAM TART
ON MAPLE SHORTBREAD COOKIE CRUST

From the maple shortbread cookie crust to the layer of sweet jam to the sliced fruit on top, this dessert is every bit as refreshing as it is sweet and celebratory. For the fruit, you could use peaches, pears, apples, apricots, or even cranberries, depending on what's in season at the time. Likewise, choose whatever jam you like best. If you wind up with leftover shortbread crust, form it into balls and bake them on a parchment-lined baking sheet right alongside the tart.

* Preheat the oven to 350°F (180°C, or gas mark 4). Generously butter a 9- or 10-inch (23 or 25 cm) round tart pan, line with parchment, and butter again.

* In a food processor, pulse together einkorn flour and salt. Add cubed butter and blend for 1 to 2 minutes, until butter is incorporated throughout. Add maple syrup; pulse until mixture starts clumping together like a ball of dough. Turn off machine, gather together the dough, and press it into your pan, into the bottom and sides (a 9-inch [23 cm] pan will have more dough up the sides; a 10-inch [25 cm] pan will be mostly pressed into the bottom). Pierce the dough gently all over with a fork. If using a springform tart pan, place the pan on top of a baking sheet and place in the oven; if using a traditional tart pan, place the pan directly in the oven. Bake for 14 to 18 minutes.

* Remove tart crust from oven when it's just slightly golden. Dollop on jam, spreading an even layer all over the crust. Top with sliced fruit, organizing them in a circular fashion, and sprinkle with a little sugar, if desired. Bake again for 3 to 6 minutes, until the jam is bubbly and the sliced fruit is just getting soft. Let cool before slicing and serving.

Yield: One 9-inch (23 cm) or 10-inch (25 cm) tart, or 8 to 10 servings

1¾ cup (219 g) all-purpose einkorn flour

½ teaspoon sea salt

½ cup (55 g) unsalted butter, cold and cubed into 8 pieces

¼ cup (60 ml) organic Grade B maple syrup

½ cup (160 g) fruit jam

2 ripe but firm fruit (such as peaches), washed and sliced into half circles

Coconut sugar or Sucanat, for sprinkling (optional)

SMALL-BATCH MINI CHERRY BANANA GALETTES

Sometimes you want a quick dessert that doesn't leave you with leftovers for days. Enter these galettes. Easy to assemble, the recipe only makes 4 mini-size galettes, each with sweet and tangy filling wrapped inside a crisp, buttery crust.

✳ Preheat the oven to 375°F (190°C, or gas mark 5) and line 2 rimmed baking sheets with parchment. In a small bowl, combine cherries, Sucanat, almond extract, lime juice, and cornstarch. Blend until everything is evenly coated. Add sliced banana, stirring gently to prevent mashing.

✳ Combine einkorn flour and salt in a medium bowl. Using a pastry cutter, cut in the cubed butter until the mixture resembles coarse crumbs. Stir in water, and then use your hands to press and form the mixture into a nice ball. Divide this dough into 4 sections. Working with one section at a time on a floured surface, roll out 5- to 6-inch (13 to 15 cm) rounds and place them on baking sheets.

✳ Divide cherry-banana mixture evenly between the 4 rounds of dough, leaving a border edge of about 2 inches (5 cm). Fold the edges up and pleat them as you do. Brush the edges of the dough with yogurt and bake for 40 to 45 minutes, until golden. Serve warm or at room temperature.

Yield: Four 4-inch (10 cm) galettes

FOR THE FILLING:

2 cups (300 g) halved, sweet cherries (fresh; or thawed, strained frozen)

¼ cup (40 g) Sucanat

2 teaspoons almond extract

1 tablespoon (15 ml) lime juice

2 tablespoons (16 g) non-GMO cornstarch (or arrowroot powder)

1 small banana, sliced into ¼-inch (6 mm) rounds

FOR THE PASTRY DOUGH:

1 cup (125 g) all-purpose einkorn flour

½ teaspoon sea salt

½ cup (112 g) unsalted butter, cold and cubed

¼ cup (60 ml) cold water

1 tablespoon (15 g) yogurt, for brushing

Recipe Note

• *The filling without the banana may be cooled for 10 to 15 minutes over medium heat to thicken before adding to the dough.*

WAFFLE BOWLS

Yield: 4 waffle bowls or cones

If there's anything better than ice cream, it's ice cream in a crisp, homemade waffle bowl. We borrowed a friend's waffle cone maker to create ours, but you could also do the same thing on a skillet: Brush the skillet with oil and warm it over medium heat until hot to the touch. Drizzle spoonfuls of batter on the skillet, spreading them with the back of a spoon until very thin. Cook until firm on bottom; flip with a spatula, then remove to a towel and form immediately, holding in place until cooled.

1 egg

1 egg white

¼ teaspoon sea salt

⅓ cup (53 g) Sucanat

½ cup (63 g) all-purpose einkorn flour

1 tablespoon (14 g) unsalted butter, melted and cooled

1 teaspoon vanilla extract

1 tablespoon (15 ml) milk

✳ Place all ingredients in a medium bowl, whisk until well combined, and let mixture rest while waffle iron preheats.

✳ When iron is ready, dollop 2 to 3 tablespoons (14 to 21 g) of batter at a time onto the iron, following the manufacturer's instructions for cook time. You know the batter is cooked when you stop seeing steam escaping out the sides.

✳ Using pot holders or towels, remove each piece and immediately begin shaping as you like. For waffle bowls, set a piece in a ramekin and place a smaller ramekin inside/on top. For cones, shape around a cone-like object or carefully use towels. After a few seconds, the bowls or cones should harden and be ready to use.

RESOURCES

Most of the ingredients found throughout this book are available at specialty grocery stores or health food chains, but buying them online can also be highly cost-effective and convenient. With that in mind, here are a few helpful resources to check out.

EINKORN

ALL-PURPOSE EINKORN FLOUR
- Jovial Foods (www.jovialfoods.com)
- Tropical Traditions (www.tropicaltraditions.com)

WHOLE-GRAIN EINKORN FLOUR
- Breadtopia (www.breadtopia.com/store/organic-einkorn-wheat-flour.html)
- GrowSeed.org (www.growseed.org/einkorn.html)
- Tropical Traditions (www.tropicaltraditions.com)

EINKORN BERRIES
- Einkorn.com (www.einkorn.com)
- Jovial Foods (www.jovialfoods.com)
- Pleasant Hill Grain (www.pleasanthillgrain.com/buy_einkorn_berries_organic_ancient_grain_wheat.aspx)
- Tropical Traditions (www.tropicaltraditions.com)

SWEETENERS

COCONUT SUGAR
- Madhava (www.madhavasweeteners.com)
- Navitas Naturals (www.navitasnaturals.com)

MAPLE SYRUP
- Square Deal Farm (www.squaredealfarm.org)

SORGHUM SYRUP
- Muddy Pond Sorghum Mill (www.muddypondsorghum.com)

SUCANAT
- Wholesome Sweeteners (www.wholesomesweeteners.com)

OTHER INGREDIENTS

ARROWROOT POWDER
- Bob's Red Mill (www.bobsredmill.com)

VANILLA BEANS
- Amazon (www.amazon.com)

ACKNOWLEDGMENTS

WITH FULL HEARTS

If there's anything you learn when you write a book, it's how much you need help—and if there's anything you learn from writing a book with your spouse, it's how much you need help from one another each day. While it's true my voice is the one you hear throughout the book, every part of this project has been collaborative, and we're so grateful for the opportunity not only to publish a collection of recipes, but also for the opportunity to do it together. I am especially grateful for the opportunity to do it with Tim, my true partner in all parts of life. Creating this cookbook has been a labor of love for us in every sense of the phrase, and we look at this finished project with full hearts, overwhelmed by the support and encouragement of so many along the way.

Thank you, Amanda Waddell, of Fair Winds Press, for setting this book in motion and carrying it through to completion with expertise and skill. We have so much respect for what you do and are so grateful to have you on our team. Thank you, Heather Godin and Renae Haines, for being so easy to work with, and to the entire team at Fair Winds for believing in our book concept and making it a reality.

We could not have assembled so many recipes so quickly without the extraordinary help of our volunteer recipe testers: Erin Alderson, Jacquie Astemborski, Carrie Barga, Elizabeth Belof, Sarah Carter, Allison Godart, Julie Grice, Lindsey Hepler, Tabitha Hindman, Elizabeth Machado, Marie Matter, Kira Miller, Heather Penn, Michele Reynolds, Angela Roberts, Wendy Ryan, MariJean Sanders, Christa Schneider, Renee Shuman, Kristin Silverman, Roxanne Spielvogel, Aimee Suen, Shannon Tompson, Sarah Keith Valentine, Lan Pham Wilson, and Micah Wixom. Thank you not only for the time, money, and energy you invested in testing our recipe drafts, but also for your ready and willing hearts to do so. People often talk about loving others with food—you loved us with your willingness to help us where we needed it most. Thank you times a million.

Nathan, Jared, Terry, and the staff of Life Fitness Academy in Nashville: Without you, we would have easily eaten our weight in einkorn week after week. Thank you for being our ready taste testers and for gladly taking our batches and batches of bread, muffins, cookies, cakes, quiches, breadsticks, and everything else. We couldn't have done this without you.

To the readers of Food Loves Writing who, at every mention of the cookbook, at every new photo on Instagram, at even the slightest mention of what we were working on, jumped up to encourage, cheer, and buoy us on with your kind words: You are the absolute best part of blogging. We hope you know this book is for you.

To our families and friends who prayed for us while we worked to meet deadlines and perfect yet another loaf of bread: There is no greater gift.

And to the sovereign God who knit our lives together and who works all things together for good: We have never been eloquent, but it is you who moves our mouths.

ABOUT THE AUTHORS

Shanna Mallon is the voice behind the personal blog Food Loves Writing, which she runs and photographs with her husband, Tim. When she started the site in 2008, it was to chronicle cooking attempts, practice writing, and remember her grandma, who had passed away nine years before. In the years that followed, she fell in love with whole foods, as well as a man, Tim, who emailed her one November night from his home in Nashville, Tennessee. Her ebook, written together, chronicles that story. Shanna holds an M.A. in writing from DePaul University, and her work has been featured in The Kitchn, BlogHer and Entrepreneur. When she's not cooking and blogging about life at FoodLovesWriting.com, she works from her Nashville home as a marketing copywriter.

Tim Mallon became interested in whole foods and nutrition when he began researching health information after his mom passed away in 2002. Discovering firsthand the beauty and power of fresh foods eaten in their original forms, he found himself fascinated by how what we eat affects our bodies and why. When he saw a Chicago food blogger writing about digestive problems, he shot her an email—and that email led to a first meeting, which led to a long-distance relationship, which led to his marriage to Shanna in October 2011. Today, he develops recipes, shoots photos, and does behind-the-scenes work on the couple's shared blog, Food Loves Writing. He also works as a manager and nutrition consultant for personal fitness studio Life Fitness Academy in Nashville.

INDEX

Acorn Squash and Caramelized Onion Salad, 89
all-purpose einkorn flour. *See also* einkorn; whole-
        grain einkorn flour.
    Apple Dumplings, 159
    Avocado Parathas, 62
    Basic Pasta Dough, 126
    Breaded Lemon Chicken with Capers on Pilaf, 114
    Butternut Squash Gnocchi with Sweet Garlic-Ginger
        Brown Butter Sauce, 128
    Cannoli Cupcakes, 139
    Cherry Walnut Sourdough Boule, 68
    Chocolate Layer Cake with Chocolate Buttercream,
        138
    Chocolate Pear Cake, 136
    Cinnamon Buns, 26
    Cinnamon Raisin Bread, 50–51
    Classic Anise Biscotti, 150
    Classic Artisan Sourdough Bread, 66–67
    Crisp and Buttery Belgian Waffles, 22
    Curried Cauliflower Puff Pies with Parsley Mint
        Chutney, 72–73
    Decadent Chocolate Chip Belgian Waffles, 23
    Dinner Rolls, 54
    Flaky All-Butter Pie Crust, 156
    flavor profile, 12, 43
    Focaccia with Caramelized Onions and Tomatoes, 56
    Fruit and Jam Tart on Maple Shortbread Cookie Crust, 163
    Fudgey Cookies, 144
    Grandma's Oatmeal Chocolate Chip Cookies, 143
    Grape and Thyme Galette, 155
    Herbed Sourdough Crackers, 81
    Honey Currant Scones, 32
    introduction, 12
    Kale and Cremini Vegetable Pot Pie, 117
    King-Size Chocolate Chip Currant Cookies, 152
    Maple Ginger Shortcakes, 141
    Marble Rye Bread, 49
    Meat and Potato Pasties, 108
    One-Bowl Butter Bread, 46
    Peach, Basil, and Ricotta Flatbreads, 75
    Pear Cinnamon Roll Muffins, 30
    Pistachio Cranberry Cookies, 149
    Potato Rosemary Dutch Baby Pancake with Roasted
        Red Pepper Sauce, 36
    Pretzel Rolls, 65
    Rosemary Breadsticks, 57
    Rosewater Sorghum Shortbread Cookies with Choco-
        late Drizzle, 154
    Rustic Apple Tartlets, 160
    Simple Homemade Tortillas, 60
    Small-Batch Mini Cherry Banana Galettes, 164
    Small-Batch Vanilla Cupcakes with Butterscotch
        Buttercream, 140
    Soft, Pillowy Pita Pockets, 59
    Soft Sandwich Loaf, 45
    Sourdough English Muffins, 29
    Sourdough Pizza Crust, 132
    Sourdough Slider Buns, 63
    Spiced Cut-Out Cookies, 145
    Spicy Chocolate Sandwich Cookies, 146
    Spinach Skillet Cornbread, 52
    Streusely Banana Bread, 40
    Thin and Crispy Pizza Crust, 130

    Tomato Pastry Tart, 84
    Vanilla Cardamom Breakfast Tea Cake, 27
    Waffle Bowls, 166
    weight, 12
almonds
    Dried Fruit and Toasted Almond Einkorn Berry Salad, 100
    Parsley Pesto Pizza, 133
    Thai Noodle Bowls, 125
appetizers
    Caramelized Onion, Mushroom, and Mozzarella
        Quesadillas, 74
    Curried Cauliflower Puff Pies with Parsley Mint
        Chutney, 72–73
    Herbed Sourdough Crackers, 81
    introduction, 71
    Lettuce Wraps with Peanut Sauce, 78
    Olive Tapenade, 82
    Peach, Basil, and Ricotta Flatbreads, 75
    Sweet Potato and Onion Crostini, 77
    Tomato Avocado Crostini, 77
    Tomato Pastry Tart, 84
apples
    Acorn Squash and Caramelized Onion Salad, 89
    Apple Dumplings, 159
    Apple Pie Breakfast Risotto, 42
    Fruit and Jam Tart on Maple Shortbread Cookie Crust, 163
    Rustic Apple Tartlets, 160
avocados
    Avocado Parathas, 62
    California-Style BLT with Roasted Garlic and
        Rosemary Yogurt Sauce, 113
    Tomato Avocado Crostini, 77

bacon
    California-Style BLT with Roasted Garlic and
        Rosemary Yogurt Sauce, 113
    Spinach Skillet Cornbread, 52
bananas
    Small-Batch Mini Cherry Banana Galettes, 164
    Streusely Banana Bread, 40
Basic Pasta Dough
    Ravioli with Sundried Tomatoes, Capers, and Ricotta, 127
    recipe, 126
beans and sprouts
    Corn and White Bean Salad, 98
    Lettuce Wraps with Peanut Sauce, 78
beef
    California-Style BLT with Roasted Garlic and
        Rosemary Yogurt Sauce, 113
    Italian Meatball Sandwiches, 110
    Meat and Potato Pasties, 108
bell peppers
    Dried Fruit and Toasted Almond Einkorn Berry Salad, 100
    Lamb-Stuffed Peppers, 123
    Meat and Potato Pasties, 108
    Ricotta Vegetable Quiche, 35
    Vegetable Lentil Stew, 118
blackberries. *See* Chocolate Layer Cake with Chocolate
        Buttercream, 138
blueberries
    Chocolate Blueberry Pie, 161
    Popped Einkorn Berry Parfaits, 39
Boyce, Kim, 152

Breaded Lemon Chicken with Capers on Pilaf, 114
breads
    Avocado Parathas, 62
    Cherry Walnut Sourdough Boule, 68
    Cinnamon Raisin Bread, 50–51
    Classic Artisan Sourdough Bread, 66–67
    Dinner Rolls, 54
    Focaccia with Caramelized Onions and Tomatoes, 56
    Garlic Cheese Sourdough Croutons, 70
    Herbed Bread Crumbs, 70
    introduction, 43
    Marble Rye Bread, 49
    One-Bowl Butter Bread, 46
    Pretzel Rolls, 65
    Rosemary Breadsticks, 57
    Simple Homemade Tortillas, 60
    Soft, Pillowy Pita Pockets, 59
    Soft Sandwich Loaf, 45
    Sourdough Slider Buns, 63
    Spinach Skillet Cornbread, 52
    Whole-Grain Dinner Rolls, 55
    Whole-Grain Sourdough, 68–69
breakfasts
    Apple Pie Breakfast Risotto, 42
    Cinnamon Buns, 26
    Cinnamon Doughnut Holes, 24
    Cranberry Orange Whole-Grain Muffins, 31
    Cream of Einkorn, 41
    Crisp and Buttery Belgian Waffles, 22
    Decadent Chocolate Chip Belgian Waffles, 23
    Honey Currant Scones, 32
    introduction, 19
    Pear Cinnamon Roll Muffins, 30
    Popped Einkorn Berry Parfaits, 39
    Potato Rosemary Dutch Baby Pancake with Roasted
        Red Pepper Sauce, 36
    Ricotta Vegetable Quiche, 35
    Sourdough English Muffins, 29
    Streusely Banana Bread, 40
    Vanilla Cardamom Breakfast Tea Cake, 27
    Whole-Grain Overnight Pancakes, 20
Brown, Alton, 82
butternut squash
    Butternut Squash Gnocchi with Sweet Garlic-Ginger
        Brown Butter Sauce, 128
    Butternut Squash Pilaf, 102

California-Style BLT with Roasted Garlic and Rosemary
        Yogurt Sauce, 113
Cannoli Cupcakes, 139
Caramelized Onion, Mushroom, and Mozzarella
        Quesadillas, 74
carrots
    Kale and Cremini Vegetable Pot Pie, 117
    Lettuce Wraps with Peanut Sauce, 78
    Meat and Potato Pasties, 108
    Vegetable Lentil Stew, 118
    Vegetable Soup with Red Wine and Lemon, 121
cauliflower. *See* Curried Cauliflower Puff Pies with Parsley
        Mint Chutney, 72–73
cheese
    Acorn Squash and Caramelized Onion Salad, 89
    Apple Pie Breakfast Risotto, 42

Breaded Lemon Chicken with Capers on Pilaf, 114
Cannoli Cupcakes, 139
Caramelized Onion, Mushroom, and Mozzarella
    Quesadillas, 74
Focaccia with Caramelized Onions and Tomatoes, 56
Garlic Cheese Sourdough Croutons, 70
Italian Meatball Sandwiches, 110
Italian-Style Kale and Einkorn Berry Salad, 92
Italian-Style Mustard Green Soup, 122
Kale and Red Pepper Risotto, 106
Lamb-Stuffed Peppers, 123
Mediterranean Salad, 99
Mushroom Salad with Crushed Red Pepper, 90
Parsley Pesto Caprese Salad, 94
Parsley Pesto Pizza, 133
Peach, Basil, and Ricotta Flatbreads, 75
Potato Rosemary Dutch Baby Pancake with Roasted
    Red Pepper Sauce, 36
Ravioli with Sundried Tomatoes, Capers, and Ricotta, 127
Red Wine Risotto, 105
Ricotta Vegetable Quiche, 35
Rosemary Breadsticks, 57
Strawberry Leek Pizza with Kefir Crust, 130–131
Stuffed Tomatoes, 134
Sweet Potato and Onion Crostini, 77
cherries
    Cherry Walnut Sourdough Boule, 68
    Small-Batch Mini Cherry Banana Galettes, 164
chicken. See Breaded Lemon Chicken with Capers on
    Pilaf, 114
chocolate
    Cannoli Cupcakes, 139
    Chocolate Blueberry Pie, 161
    Chocolate Layer Cake with Chocolate Buttercream, 138
    Chocolate Pear Cake, 136
    Classic Anise Biscotti, 150
    Decadent Chocolate Chip Belgian Waffles, 23
    Fudgey Cookies, 144
    Grandma's Oatmeal Chocolate Chip Cookies, 143
    King-Size Chocolate Chip Currant Cookies, 152
    Rosewater Sorghum Shortbread Cookies with Choco-
        late Drizzle, 154
    Spicy Chocolate Sandwich Cookies, 146
chromosomes, 10
Cinnamon Buns, 26
Cinnamon Doughnut Holes, 24
Cinnamon Raisin Bread, 50–51
Classic Anise Biscotti, 150
Classic Artisan Sourdough Bread
    Classic Panzanella, 95
    Radish Panzanella, 97
    recipe, 66–67
coconut oil
    Acorn Squash and Caramelized Onion Salad, 89
    Avocado Parathas, 62
    Breaded Lemon Chicken with Capers on Pilaf, 114
    Butternut Squash Gnocchi with Sweet Garlic-Ginger
        Brown Butter Sauce, 128
    Butternut Squash Pilaf, 102
    Caramelized Onion, Mushroom, and Mozzarella
        Quesadillas, 74
    Chocolate Layer Cake with Chocolate Buttercream, 138
    Cinnamon Doughnut Holes, 24
    Curried Cauliflower Puff Pies with Parsley Mint
        Chutney, 72–73
    Focaccia with Caramelized Onions and Tomatoes, 56
    Fudgey Cookies, 144
    Grandma's Oatmeal Chocolate Chip Cookies, 143
    Herbed Sourdough Crackers, 81
    introduction, 16
    Kale and Cremini Vegetable Pot Pie, 117

Kale and Red Pepper Risotto, 106
Lamb-Stuffed Peppers, 123
Meat and Potato Pasties, 108
Mushroom Salad with Crushed Red Pepper, 90
Potato Rosemary Dutch Baby Pancake with Roasted
    Red Pepper Sauce, 36
Ricotta Vegetable Quiche, 35
Simple Homemade Tortillas, 60
Soft Sandwich Loaf, 45
Sourdough English Muffins, 29
Spicy Chocolate Sandwich Cookies, 146
Strawberry Leek Pizza with Kefir Crust, 130–131
Vanilla Cardamom Breakfast Tea Cake, 27
Vegetable Lentil Stew, 118
Vegetable Soup with Red Wine and Lemon, 121
Whole-Grain Overnight Pancakes, 20
coconut sugar
    Butternut Squash Gnocchi with Sweet Garlic-Ginger
        Brown Butter Sauce, 128
    Cannoli Cupcakes, 139
    Chocolate Blueberry Pie, 161
    Chocolate Layer Cake with Chocolate Buttercream, 138
    Chocolate Pear Cake, 136
    Cinnamon Buns, 26
    Cinnamon Doughnut Holes, 24
    Cinnamon Raisin Bread, 50–51
    Classic Anise Biscotti, 150
    Cranberry Orange Whole-Grain Muffins, 31
    Curried Cauliflower Puff Pies with Parsley Mint
        Chutney, 72–73
    Decadent Chocolate Chip Belgian Waffles, 23
    Fruit and Jam Tart on Maple Shortbread Cookie Crust, 163
    Fudgey Cookies, 144
    Grape and Thyme Galette, 155
    introduction, 16
    King-Size Chocolate Chip Currant Cookies, 152
    Pear Cinnamon Roll Muffins, 30
    Potato Rosemary Dutch Baby Pancake with Roasted
        Red Pepper Sauce, 36
    Rosemary Breadsticks, 57
    Small-Batch Vanilla Cupcakes with Butterscotch
        Buttercream, 140
    Sourdough Slider Buns, 63
    Spiced Cut-Out Cookies, 145
    Spicy Salmon Over Cilantro Lime Einkorn, 111
    Spinach Skillet Cornbread, 52
    Streusely Banana Bread, 40
    Whole-Grain Overnight Pancakes, 20
Cooked Einkorn Berries
    Acorn Squash and Caramelized Onion Salad, 89
    Breaded Lemon Chicken with Capers on Pilaf, 114
    Butternut Squash Pilaf, 102
    Italian-Style Kale and Einkorn Berry Salad, 92
    Italian-Style Mustard Green Soup, 122
    Lamb-Stuffed Peppers, 123
    Lettuce Wraps with Peanut Sauce, 78
    Mediterranean Salad, 99
    Olive Tapenade, 82
    Parsley Pesto Caprese Salad, 94
    recipe, 15
    Spicy Salmon Over Cilantro Lime Einkorn, 111
    Stuffed Tomatoes, 134
    Vegetable Soup with Red Wine and Lemon, 121
corn
    Corn and White Bean Salad, 98
    Spinach Skillet Cornbread, 52
cranberries
    Cranberry Orange Whole-Grain Muffins, 31
    Fruit and Jam Tart on Maple Shortbread Cookie Crust, 163
    Pistachio Cranberry Cookies, 149
cream cheese. See Rosemary Breadsticks, 57

Cream of Einkorn, 41
Crisp and Buttery Belgian Waffles, 22
cucumbers
    Classic Panzanella, 95
    Lettuce Wraps with Peanut Sauce, 78
    Tabbouleh, 87
currants
    Apple Dumplings, 159
    Honey Currant Scones, 32
    King-Size Chocolate Chip Currant Cookies, 152
Curried Cauliflower Puff Pies with Parsley Mint Chutney, 72–73

dates. See Dried Fruit and Toasted Almond Einkorn Berry
    Salad, 100
Decadent Chocolate Chip Belgian Waffles, 23
desserts
    Apple Dumplings, 159
    Cannoli Cupcakes, 139
    Chocolate Blueberry Pie, 161
    Chocolate Layer Cake with Chocolate Buttercream, 138
    Chocolate Pear Cake, 136
    Classic Anise Biscotti, 150
    Flaky All-Butter Pie Crust, 156
    Fruit and Jam Tart on Maple Shortbread Cookie Crust, 163
    Fudgey Cookies, 144
    Grandma's Oatmeal Chocolate Chip Cookies, 143
    Grape and Thyme Galette, 155
    Hearty Whole-Grain Pie Crust, 157
    introduction, 135
    King-Size Chocolate Chip Currant Cookies, 152
    Maple Ginger Shortcakes, 141
    Pistachio Cranberry Cookies, 149
    Rosewater Sorghum Shortbread Cookies with Choco-
        late Drizzle, 154
    Rustic Apple Tartlets, 160
    Small-Batch Mini Cherry Banana Galettes, 164
    Small-Batch Vanilla Cupcakes with Butterscotch But-
        tercream, 140
    Spiced Cut-Out Cookies, 145
    Spicy Chocolate Sandwich Cookies, 146
    Waffle Bowls, 166
Dinner Rolls, 54
dough scrapers, 17
dressings
    Dried Fruit and Toasted Almond Einkorn Berry Salad, 100
    Italian-Style Kale and Einkorn Berry Salad, 92
    Mediterannean Salad, 99
Dried Fruit and Toasted Almond Einkorn Berry Salad, 100

einkorn berries
    Acorn Squash and Caramelized Onion Salad, 89
    Apple Pie Breakfast Risotto, 42
    Breaded Lemon Chicken with Capers on Pilaf, 114
    Butternut Squash Pilaf, 102
    cooking, 15
    Corn and White Bean Salad, 98
    Cream of Einkorn, 41
    Dried Fruit and Toasted Almond Einkorn Berry Salad, 100
    Herbed Tomato Salad, 91
    Italian-Style Kale and Einkorn Berry Salad, 92
    Italian-Style Mustard Green Soup, 122
    Kale and Red Pepper Risotto, 106
    Lamb-Stuffed Peppers, 123
    Lettuce Wraps with Peanut Sauce, 78
    Mediterranean Salad, 99
    Mushroom Salad with Crushed Red Pepper, 90
    Olive Tapenade, 82
    Parsley Pesto Caprese Salad, 94
    Popped Einkorn Berry Parfaits, 39
    Red Wine Risotto, 105
    soaking, 14

Spicy Salmon Over Cilantro Lime Einkorn, 111
sprouting, 14
storing, 13
Stuffed Tomatoes, 134
Tabbouleh, 87
Vegetable Lentil Stew, 118
Vegetable Soup with Red Wine and Lemon, 121
Einkorn.com website, 13
einkorn flour. *See also* all-purpose einkorn flour; whole-
    grain einkorn flour.
    chromosomes, 10
    cooking with, 11
    cost, 13
    digestibility, 10, 14
    gluten, 15
    history, 10, 11
    introduction, 9
    making at home, 14
    names of, 11
    nutritional value, 9, 10
    purchasing, 13
    root system, 9
    soaking, 14
    sprouted, 12
    storing, 13
    taste of, 12, 43
    weights, 12

Fallon, Sally, 14
Flaky All-Butter Pie Crust
    Chocolate Blueberry Pie, 161
    Kale and Cremini Vegetable Pot Pie, 117
    recipe, 156
    Ricotta Vegetable Quiche, 35
Focaccia with Caramelized Onions and Tomatoes, 56
food processors, 17
Forte, Sarah, 130
Fruit and Jam Tart on Maple Shortbread Cookie Crust, 163
Fudgey Cookies, 144

garlic
    Breaded Lemon Chicken with Capers on Pilaf, 114
    Butternut Squash Gnocchi with Sweet Garlic-Ginger
        Brown Butter Sauce, 128
    California-Style BLT with Roasted Garlic and Rose-
        mary Yogurt Sauce, 113
    Corn and White Bean Salad, 98
    Focaccia with Caramelized Onions and Tomatoes, 56
    Garlic Cheese Sourdough Croutons, 70
    Italian Meatball Sandwiches, 110
    Italian-Style Kale and Einkorn Berry Salad, 92
    Italian-Style Mustard Green Soup, 122
    Lamb-Stuffed Peppers, 123
    Lettuce Wraps with Peanut Sauce, 78
    Parsley Pesto Caprese Salad, 94
    Parsley Pesto Pizza, 133
    Spicy Salmon Over Cilantro Lime Einkorn, 111
    Tabbouleh, 87
    Tomato Avocado Crostini, 77
    Vegetable Soup with Red Wine and Lemon, 121
ghee
    Apple Pie Breakfast Risotto, 42
    Cinnamon Buns, 26
    Herbed Sourdough Crackers, 81
    introduction, 16
    Spicy Salmon Over Cilantro Lime Einkorn, 111
    Sweet Potato and Onion Crostini, 77
    Tomato Avocado Crostini, 77
gluten, 10, 15, 66
goat cheese. *See* Mediterranean Salad, 99
Good to the Grain (Kim Boyce), 152

grain mills, 17
Grandma's Oatmeal Chocolate Chip Cookies, 143
Grape and Thyme Galette, 155
GrowSeed.org website, 13

Hazan, Marcella, 110
hazelnuts
    Pear Cinnamon Roll Muffins, 30
    Rustic Apple Tartlets, 160
Hearty Whole-Grain Pie Crust
    Chocolate Blueberry Pie, 161
    recipe, 157
    Ricotta Vegetable Quiche, 35
Herbed Bread Crumbs
    Italian Meatball Sandwiches, 110
    Italian-Style Kale and Einkorn Berry Salad, 92
    Lamb-Stuffed Peppers, 123
    recipe, 70
    Stuffed Tomatoes, 134
Herbed Sourdough Crackers, 81
Herbed Tomato Salad, 91
honey
    Cinnamon Buns, 26
    Cinnamon Raisin Bread, 50–51
    Classic Artisan Sourdough Bread, 66–67
    Cream of Einkorn, 41
    Dinner Rolls, 54
    Focaccia with Caramelized Onions and Tomatoes, 56
    Honey Currant Scones, 32
    Lettuce Wraps with Peanut Sauce, 78
    Marble Rye Bread, 49
    Mediterranean Salad, 99
    Peach, Basil, and Ricotta Flatbreads, 75
    Peanut Sauce, 78
    Popped Einkorn Berry Parfaits, 39
    Pretzel Rolls, 65
    Rosemary Breadsticks, 57
    Rustic Apple Tartlets, 160
    Soft, Pillowy Pita Pockets, 59
    Soft Sandwich Loaf, 45
    Sourdough Slider Buns, 63
    Spinach Skillet Cornbread, 52
    Whole-Grain Dinner Rolls, 55
    Whole-Grain Sourdough, 68–69

Italian Meatball Sandwiches, 110
Italian-Style Kale and Einkorn Berry Salad, 92
Italian-Style Mustard Green Soup, 122

Journal of Gastroenterology, 10

kale
    Italian-Style Kale and Einkorn Berry Salad, 92
    Kale and Cremini Vegetable Pot Pie, 117
    Kale and Red Pepper Risotto, 106
    Vegetable Lentil Stew, 118
    Vegetable Soup with Red Wine and Lemon, 121
kefir
    Chocolate Blueberry Pie, 161
    Cinnamon Raisin Bread, 50–51
    Decadent Chocolate Chip Belgian Waffles, 23
    introduction, 16
    Pear Cinnamon Roll Muffins, 30
    Strawberry Leek Pizza with Kefir Crust, 130–131
    Thin and Crispy Pizza Crust, 130
    Whole-Grain Overnight Pancakes, 20
King-Size Chocolate Chip Currant Cookies, 152

Lamb-Stuffed Peppers, 123
leeks. *See* Strawberry Leek Pizza with Kefir Crust, 130–131
lemon

Avocado Parathas, 62
Breaded Lemon Chicken with Capers on Pilaf, 114
Cannoli Cupcakes, 139
Chocolate Blueberry Pie, 161
Corn and White Bean Salad, 98
Curried Cauliflower Puff Pies with Parsley Mint
    Chutney, 72–73
Dried Fruit and Toasted Almond Einkorn Berry Salad, 100
Italian-Style Kale and Einkorn Berry Salad, 92
Mediterranean Salad, 99
Mint Chutney, 73
Parsley Pesto Pizza, 133
Radish Panzanella, 97
Rustic Apple Tartlets, 160
Tabbouleh, 87
Vegetable Soup with Red Wine and Lemon, 121
lentils. *See* Vegetable Lentil Stew, 118
lettuce
    California-Style BLT with Roasted Garlic and
        Rosemary Yogurt Sauce, 113
    Lettuce Wraps with Peanut Sauce, 78
lime juice
    Grape and Thyme Galette, 155
    Small-Batch Mini Cherry Banana Galettes, 164
    Spicy Salmon Over Cilantro Lime Einkorn, 111

main dishes
    Basic Pasta Dough, 126
    Breaded Lemon Chicken with Capers on Pilaf, 114
    Butternut Squash Gnocchi with Sweet Garlic-Ginger
        Brown Butter Sauce, 128
    California-Style BLT with Roasted Garlic and
        Rosemary Yogurt Sauce, 113
    introduction, 103
    Italian Meatball Sandwiches, 110
    Italian-Style Mustard Green Soup, 122
    Kale and Cremini Vegetable Pot Pie, 117
    Kale and Red Pepper Risotto, 106
    Lamb-Stuffed Peppers, 123
    Meat and Potato Pasties, 108
    Parsley Pesto Pizza, 133
    Ravioli with Sundried Tomatoes, Capers, and Ricotta, 127
    Red Wine Risotto, 105
    Sourdough Pizza Crust, 132
    Spicy Salmon Over Cilantro Lime Einkorn, 111
    Strawberry Leek Pizza with Kefir Crust, 130–131
    Stuffed Tomatoes, 134
    Thai Noodle Bowls, 125
    Thin and Crispy Pizza Crust, 130
    Vegetable Lentil Stew, 118
    Vegetable Soup with Red Wine and Lemon, 121
    Whole-Grain Egg Noodles, 124
maple syrup
    Cream of Einkorn, 41
    Crisp and Buttery Belgian Waffles, 22
    Decadent Chocolate Chip Belgian Waffles, 23
    Fruit and Jam Tart on Maple Shortbread Cookie Crust, 163
    Fudgey Cookies, 144
    introduction, 16
    Maple Ginger Shortcakes, 141
    Pear Cinnamon Roll Muffins, 30
    Rosewater Sorghum Shortbread Cookies with Choco-
        late Drizzle, 154
    Whole-Grain Overnight Pancakes, 20
Marble Rye Bread
    California-Style BLT with Roasted Garlic and Rose-
        mary Yogurt Sauce, 113
    recipe, 49
Meat and Potato Pasties, 108
Mediterranean Salad, 99
medium chain triglycerides (MCTs), 16

milk
Apple Pie Breakfast Risotto, 42
Cannoli Cupcakes, 139
Cinnamon Raisin Bread, 50–51
Cranberry Orange Whole-Grain Muffins, 31
Cream of Einkorn, 41
Crisp and Buttery Belgian Waffles, 22
Decadent Chocolate Chip Belgian Waffles, 23
Dinner Rolls, 54
Honey Currant Scones, 32
introduction, 17
Italian Meatball Sandwiches, 110
Kale and Cremini Vegetable Pot Pie, 117
King-Size Chocolate Chip Currant Cookies, 152
Marble Rye Bread, 49
Pear Cinnamon Roll Muffins, 30
Potato Rosemary Dutch Baby Pancake with Roasted
Red Pepper Sauce, 36
Ricotta Vegetable Quiche, 35
Small-Batch Vanilla Cupcakes with Butterscotch
Buttercream, 140
Soft Sandwich Loaf, 45
Sourdough English Muffins, 29
Vanilla Cardamom Breakfast Tea Cake, 27
Waffle Bowls, 166
Whole-Grain Dinner Rolls, 55
Whole-Grain Overnight Pancakes, 20
mint
Lamb-Stuffed Peppers, 123
Mint Chutney, 73
Tabbouleh, 87
molasses
Fudgey Cookies, 144
Marble Rye Bread, 49
Pistachio Cranberry Cookies, 149
Spiced Cut-Out Cookies, 145
mozzarella cheese
Caramelized Onion, Mushroom, and Mozzarella
Quesadillas, 74
Parsley Pesto Caprese Salad, 94
Parsley Pesto Pizza, 133
Strawberry Leek Pizza with Kefir Crust, 130–131
mushrooms
Caramelized Onion, Mushroom, and Mozzarella
Quesadillas, 74
Kale and Cremini Vegetable Pot Pie, 117
Mushroom Salad with Crushed Red Pepper, 90
Ricotta Vegetable Quiche, 35
Mushroom Salad with Crushed Red Pepper, 90
mustard greens. See Italian-Style Mustard Green Soup, 122

Nourishing Traditions (Sally Fallon), 14

oats. See Grandma's Oatmeal Chocolate Chip Cookies, 143
olives
Mediterranean Salad, 99
Olive Tapenade, 82
One-Bowl Butter Bread
recipe, 46
Sweet Potato and Onion Crostini, 77
Tomato Avocado Crostini, 77
onions
Acorn Squash and Caramelized Onion Salad, 89
Breaded Lemon Chicken with Capers on Pilaf, 114
Caramelized Onion, Mushroom, and Mozzarella
Quesadillas, 74
Classic Panzanella, 95
Curried Cauliflower Puff Pies with Parsley Mint
Chutney, 72–73
Focaccia with Caramelized Onions and Tomatoes, 56
Herbed Tomato Salad, 91

Italian Meatball Sandwiches, 110
Italian-Style Mustard Green Soup, 122
Kale and Cremini Vegetable Pot Pie, 117
Kale and Red Pepper Risotto, 106
Lamb-Stuffed Peppers, 123
Meat and Potato Pasties, 108
Radish Panzanella, 97
Ravioli with Sundried Tomatoes, Capers, and Ricotta, 127
Red Wine Risotto, 105
Ricotta Vegetable Quiche, 35
Stuffed Tomatoes, 134
Sweet Potato and Onion Crostini, 77
Thai Noodle Bowls, 125
Vegetable Lentil Stew, 118
Vegetable Soup with Red Wine and Lemon, 121
oranges. See Cranberry Orange Whole-Grain Muffins, 31

parsley
Acorn Squash and Caramelized Onion Salad, 89
Butternut Squash Pilaf, 102
Corn and White Bean Salad, 98
Focaccia with Caramelized Onions and Tomatoes, 56
Garlic Cheese Sourdough Croutons, 70
Herbed Tomato Salad, 91
Italian Meatball Sandwiches, 110
Mint Chutney, 73
Mushroom Salad with Crushed Red Pepper, 90
Olive Tapenade, 82
Parsley Almond Pesto, 133
Parsley Pesto Caprese Salad, 94
Parsley Pesto Pizza, 133
Radish Panzanella, 97
Stuffed Tomatoes, 134
Tabbouleh, 87
Thai Noodle Bowls, 125
Vegetable Soup with Red Wine and Lemon, 121
pastry cutters, 17
peaches
Fruit and Jam Tart on Maple Shortbread Cookie Crust, 163
Peach, Basil, and Ricotta Flatbreads, 75
peanut butter. See Lettuce Wraps with Peanut Sauce, 78
pears
Chocolate Pear Cake, 136
Fruit and Jam Tart on Maple Shortbread Cookie Crust, 163
Pear Cinnamon Roll Muffins, 30
pecans
Apple Dumplings, 159
Apple Pie Breakfast Risotto, 42
Fudgey Cookies, 144
Pecorino cheese
Acorn Squash and Caramelized Onion Salad, 89
Breaded Lemon Chicken with Capers on Pilaf, 114
Focaccia with Caramelized Onions and Tomatoes, 56
Garlic Cheese Sourdough Croutons, 70
Italian Meatball Sandwiches, 110
Italian-Style Kale and Einkorn Berry Salad, 92
Italian-Style Mustard Green Soup, 122
Kale and Red Pepper Risotto, 106
Lamb-Stuffed Peppers, 123
Mushroom Salad with Crushed Red Pepper, 90
Parsley Pesto Caprese Salad, 94
Parsley Pesto Pizza, 133
Potato Rosemary Dutch Baby Pancake with Roasted
Red Pepper Sauce, 36
Red Wine Risotto, 105
Rosemary Breadsticks, 57
peppers
Avocado Parathas, 62
Kale and Red Pepper Risotto, 106
Mediterranean Salad, 99
Mushroom Salad with Crushed Red Pepper, 90

Roasted Red Pepper Sauce, 36
Thai Noodle Bowls, 125
Vegetable Soup with Red Wine and Lemon, 121
phytic acid, 14
pistachios
Cannoli Cupcakes, 139
Pistachio Cranberry Cookies, 149
pizza stones, 18
Popped Einkorn Berry Parfaits, 39
potatoes
Acorn Squash and Caramelized Onion Salad, 89
Meat and Potato Pasties, 108
Potato Rosemary Dutch Baby Pancake with Roasted
Red Pepper Sauce, 36
Sweet Potato and Onion Crostini, 77
Pretzel Rolls, 65
radishes
Radish Panzanella, 97
Vegetable Soup with Red Wine and Lemon, 121
raisins
Cinnamon Raisin Bread, 50
Dried Fruit and Toasted Almond Einkorn Berry Salad, 100
raspberries. See Popped Einkorn Berry Parfaits, 39
Ravioli with Sundried Tomatoes, Capers, and Ricotta, 127
red peppers
Avocado Parathas, 62
Kale and Red Pepper Risotto, 106
Mushroom Salad with Crushed Red Pepper, 90
Roasted Red Pepper Sauce, 36
Thai Noodle Bowls, 125
Red Wine Risotto, 105
ricotta cheese
Apple Pie Breakfast Risotto, 42
Cannoli Cupcakes, 139
Peach, Basil, and Ricotta Flatbreads, 75
Ravioli with Sundried Tomatoes, Capers, and Ricotta, 127
Ricotta Vegetable Quiche, 35
Stuffed Tomatoes, 134
Sweet Potato and Onion Crostini, 77
Roasted Red Pepper Sauce, 36
Rosemary Breadsticks, 57
Rosemary Yogurt Sauce, 113
Rosewater Sorghum Shortbread Cookies with Chocolate
Drizzle, 154
Rustic Apple Tartlets, 160
rye flour. See Marble Rye Bread, 49

salads
Acorn Squash and Caramelized Onion Salad, 89
Butternut Squash Pilaf, 102
Classic Panzanella, 95
Corn and White Bean Salad, 98
Dried Fruit and Toasted Almond Einkorn Berry Salad, 100
Herbed Tomato Salad, 91
introduction, 85
Italian-Style Kale and Einkorn Berry Salad, 92
Mediterranean Salad, 99
Mushroom Salad with Crushed Red Pepper, 90
Parsley Pesto Caprese Salad, 94
Radish Panzanella, 97
Tabbouleh, 87
salmon. See Spicy Salmon Over Cilantro Lime Einkorn, 111
salsa. See Spicy Salmon Over Cilantro Lime Einkorn, 111
sauces
Italian Meatball Sandwiches, 110
Parsley Almond Pesto, 133
Peanut Sauce, 78
Roasted Red Pepper Sauce, 36
Rosemary Yogurt Sauce, 113
Spicy Salmon Over Cilantro Lime Einkorn, 111

Sweet Garlic-Ginger Brown Butter Sauce, 128
scallions. *See* Lettuce Wraps with Peanut Sauce, 78
Simple Homemade Tortillas
    Caramelized Onion, Mushroom, and Mozzarella
        Quesadillas, 74
    recipe, 60
Simple Origins website, 13
Small-Batch Mini Cherry Banana Galettes, 164
Small-Batch Vanilla Cupcakes with Butterscotch
    Buttercream, 140
Soft, Pillowy Pita Pockets, 59
Soft Sandwich Loaf
    Herbed Bread Crumbs, 70
    Italian Meatball Sandwiches, 110
    recipe, 45
sorghum syrup
    introduction, 17
    Rosewater Sorghum Shortbread Cookies with
        Chocolate Drizzle, 154
soups and stews
    Italian-Style Mustard Green Soup, 122
    Vegetable Lentil Stew, 118
    Vegetable Soup with Red Wine and Lemon, 121
Sourdough English Muffins, 29
Sourdough Pizza Crust
    Parsley Pesto Pizza, 133
    recipe, 132
Sourdough Slider Buns, 63
Spiced Cut-Out Cookies, 145
Spicy Chocolate Sandwich Cookies, 146
Spicy Salmon Over Cilantro Lime Einkorn, 111
spinach
    Caramelized Onion, Mushroom, and Mozzarella
        Quesadillas, 74
    Curried Cauliflower Puff Pies with Parsley Mint
        Chutney, 72–73
    Mediterranean Salad, 99
    Ricotta Vegetable Quiche, 35
    Spinach Skillet Cornbread, 52
    Vegetable Lentil Stew, 118
sprouted einkorn flour, 12
Sprouted Kitchen, 130
Strawberry Leek Pizza with Kefir Crust, 130–131
Streusely Banana Bread, 40
Stuffed Tomatoes, 134
Sucanat
    Apple Dumplings, 159
    Cannoli Cupcakes, 139
    Cherry Walnut Sourdough Boule, 68
    Cinnamon Buns, 26
    Cranberry Orange Whole-Grain Muffins, 31
    Cream of Einkorn, 41
    Curried Cauliflower Puff Pies with Parsley Mint
        Chutney, 72–73
    Fruit and Jam Tart on Maple Shortbread Cookie Crust, 163
    Grandma's Oatmeal Chocolate Chip Cookies, 143
    introduction, 17
    Pistachio Cranberry Cookies, 149
    Potato Rosemary Dutch Baby Pancake with Roasted
        Red Pepper Sauce, 36
    Rosemary Breadsticks, 57
    Small-Batch Mini Cherry Banana Galettes, 164
    Spiced Cut-Out Cookies, 145
    Spicy Chocolate Sandwich Cookies, 146
    Spicy Salmon Over Cilantro Lime Einkorn, 111
    Streusely Banana Bread, 40
    Vanilla Cardamom Breakfast Tea Cake, 27
    Waffle Bowls, 166
    Whole-Grain Overnight Pancakes, 20
Sweet Garlic-Ginger Brown Butter Sauce, 128
sweet potatoes

Acorn Squash and Caramelized Onion Salad, 89
    Sweet Potato and Onion Crostini, 77

Tabbouleh, 87
Thai Noodle Bowls, 125
Theoretical and Applied Genetics journal, 10
Thin and Crispy Pizza Crust
    recipe, 130
    Strawberry Leek Pizza with Kefir Crust, 130–131
tomatoes
    California-Style BLT with Roasted Garlic and
        Rosemary Yogurt Sauce, 113
    Classic Panzanella, 95
    Focaccia with Caramelized Onions and Tomatoes, 56
    Herbed Tomato Salad, 91
    Italian Meatball Sandwiches, 110
    Lamb-Stuffed Peppers, 123
    Parsley Pesto Caprese Salad, 94
    Parsley Pesto Pizza, 133
    Radish Panzanella, 97
    Ravioli with Sundried Tomatoes, Capers, and Ricotta, 127
    Ricotta Vegetable Quiche, 35
    Spicy Salmon Over Cilantro Lime Einkorn, 111
    Stuffed Tomatoes, 134
    Tabbouleh, 87
    Tomato Avocado Crostini, 77
    Tomato Pastry Tart, 84
tools
    Classic Artisan Sourdough Bread, 66
    dough scrapers, 17
    food processors, 17
    grain mills, 17
    pastry cutters, 17
    pizza stones, 18
    Vitamix blenders, 18
Tropical Traditions website, 13
turnips. *See* Vegetable Soup with Red Wine and Lemon, 121
Vanilla Cardamom Breakfast Tea Cake, 27
Vegetable Lentil Stew, 118
Vegetable Soup with Red Wine and Lemon, 121
Vitamix blenders, 18

Waffle Bowls, 166
walnuts. *See* Cherry Walnut Sourdough Boule, 68
websites
    Breadtopia, 13
    Einkorn.com, 13
    Food Loves Writing blog, 8
    GrowSeed.org, 13
    Jovial Foods, 13
    Simple Origins, 13
    Tropical Traditions, 13
Whole-Grain Egg Noodles
    recipe, 124
    Thai Noodle Bowls, 125
whole-grain einkorn flour. *See also* all-purpose einkorn
        flour; einkorn flour.
    Cinnamon Doughnut Holes, 24
    Cranberry Orange Whole-Grain Muffins, 31
    Curried Cauliflower Puff Pies with Parsley Mint
        Chutney, 72–73
    flavor profiles, 12, 43
    Hearty Whole-Grain Pie Crust, 157
    introduction, 12
    Small-Batch Vanilla Cupcakes with Butterscotch
        Buttercream, 140
    Soft Sandwich Loaf, 45
    weight, 12
    Whole-Grain Dinner Rolls, 55
    Whole-Grain Egg Noodles, 124
    Whole-Grain Overnight Pancakes, 20

Whole-Grain Sourdough Bread
    Classic Panzanella, 95
    Radish Panzanella, 97
    recipe, 68–69
wine
    Red Wine Risotto, 105
    Vegetable Soup with Red Wine and Lemon, 121

yogurt
    Apple Dumplings, 159
    California-Style BLT with Roasted Garlic and
        Rosemary Yogurt Sauce, 113
    Cannoli Cupcakes, 139
    Chocolate Blueberry Pie, 161
    Chocolate Layer Cake with Chocolate Buttercream, 138
    Cinnamon Buns, 26
    Grape and Thyme Galette, 155
    Honey Currant Scones, 32
    introduction, 17
    Maple Ginger Shortcakes, 141
    Meat and Potato Pasties, 108
    Popped Einkorn Berry Parfaits, 39
    Small-Batch Mini Cherry Banana Galettes, 164
    Small-Batch Vanilla Cupcakes with Butterscotch
        Buttercream, 140
    Spinach Skillet Cornbread, 52
    Streusely Banana Bread, 40
    Thin and Crispy Pizza Crust, 130
    Tomato Pastry Tart, 84
    Whole-Grain Overnight Pancakes, 20

ALSO AVAILABLE

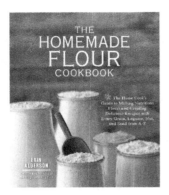

The Homemade Flour Cookbook
978-1-59233-600-5

The Healthy Coconut Flour Cookbook
978-1-59233-546-6

Back to Butter
978-1-59233-587-9

The Kitchen Pantry Cookbook
978-1-59253-843-0

CPSIA information can be obtained
at www.ICGtesting.com
Printed in the USA
LVOW05s2350091216
516592LV00004B/4/P